AF380109

Following Sarah

Robert E. Davis

Following Sarah

Sarah Davis's 1849-1850 Journey
from Michigan to California

Quiet Creek Corporation, Publishers
Twentynine Palms, California

Robert Davis is the great-great grandson of Sarah Davis. He graduated from the University of Utah in 1983 with a Bachelor of Science degree in geography. He then spent twenty-five years in the Marine Corps, retiring from active service in 2008. In 2006 he received a Master of Arts degree in National Security and Strategic Studies from the United States Naval War College in Newport, Rhode Island.

© 2013 Robert E. Davis
Quiet Creek Corporation, Publishers.
PO Box 6060, Twentynine Palms, CA 92278
sales@thequietcreek.com

ISBN-13: 978-0-9883696-0-3
ISBN-10: 0988369605

Library of Congress Control Number: 2012921121

To Carolyn and John (Davis) Sutter, the
great-great-great grandchildren of Sarah
(Green) Davis.

Table of Contents

List of Maps

List of Figures

Cover: Huntington Valley, Nevada. This photo is of the Hastings Cutoff trail west of Hastings (Overland) Pass.

Preface

My interest in my great-great grandparents' emigrant trip to California began one day when my wife pointed out that a diary written on that trip by Sarah Green Davis, my great-great grandmother, was included in Kenneth L. Holmes's *Covered Wagon Women* series. After expressing an interest on the subject to other family members, my sister sent me a copy of Sarah's diary, transcribed by Sarah's granddaughter, Minerva Power. The differences between these two transcriptions, Holmes and Power, led me to the original diary at the Yale Collection of Western Americana, Beinecke Rare Book and Manuscript Library — a digital scan of which was sent to me. Using Sarah's original script, I transcribed a third version of Sarah's diary — the heart of this volume. (There is another transcription at the Searls Library in Nevada City, California. This "fourth" transcription may have been a version of Power's, though it does not contain any information about when or by whom it was transcribed.)

It is worth noting that Sarah's diary is featured prominently in two books; the National Park Service uses it to describe portions of the National Trails System; the United States Forest Service used a picture of Sarah and a short description of her journey to promote their Big Bend Emigrant museum; several parties, including various websites, use parts of her diary for various purposes; and there is a picket line of steel guide posts across Nevada and Utah with quotes from her diary etched upon them. As emigrant diaries go, Sarah's is far from obscure.

One would think this lack of obscurity would result in a published study that provides a day-to-day analysis of where she was for each entry — a map. No such careful analysis exists. Yet, almost every page of Sarah's diary contains a geographic clue: a mileage traveled, a place name, a description of a physical feature, a type of plant or animal, or the weather that could be used as the basis of an analysis. These clues, combined with Sarah's careful record of dates, allowed me to illustrate her experience by linking her diary entries to the geography she traveled through. For example, Sarah's account of eating snow in late July is easier to grasp when we know she was traveling through today's central Wyoming, at an elevation well over 7,000 feet, near the extreme northern latitude of her trip, and traveling in a particularly cold year of the "Little Ice Age." The image of the lush grass and cold streams Sarah described in September is fuller when we know she was in the stream-fed grasslands along the eastern shoulder of Nevada's Ruby Mountains. The "color" in Sarah's diary becomes richer when placed in a geographical context.

Sarah wasn't the only one who penned thoughts in the small notebook containing her diary. The first several pages of the notebook are a collection of dated notes written by Sarah's husband, Zeno. These notes provide the few details of Zeno's aborted 1849 California trip and also help describe the travels of Sarah and Zeno between March 1849 and May 1850, the fourteen months prior to their starting the "covered wagon" portion of their journey. The details of these travels are few, so my analysis of their trips between their home in Young's Prairie, Michigan, and the St. Joseph, Missouri, area (specifically, Kingston, Missouri, where they started west in a covered wagon) is based largely on conjecture and my rudimentary understanding of the transportation systems available at the time in the United States.

Included in this book are six chapters detailing Sarah's complete trip: the Introduction, which accounts for her travels from Young's Prairie to Kingston, Missouri; the Great Plains; the "Rockey" Mountains; the Great Basin; the Sierra Nevada; and an epilogue. This chapter organization loosely corresponds to the physiographic divisions of the United States: the Central Lowlands, the Great Plains, the Rocky Mountains, the Great Basin, and the Pacific Mountains. With the exception of the Sierra Nevada chapter and epilogue, each of these chapters describes about five or six hundred miles traveled. The Sierra Nevada chapter is shorter, with less than one hundred miles covered in California. I organized the content of these chapters by the dates of Sarah's diary entries. Directly after each date is her diary entry in bold italics corresponding to the date. Following her diary entry are my explanation of Sarah's geographic position and any notes to aid the reader.

Also included are twenty-nine maps of various scales—the combination of which circumscribe Sarah's entire trip. An overview map opening each chapter depicts that chapter's portion of the trip. Several detailed maps follow, each covering about five or six days of travel. The details of her trip between Young's Prairie and Kingston are too few to support the more detailed maps, so only the overview map is included in the first chapter.

These maps are based on publicly available Geographical Information System (GIS) data provided by the United States

Geological Survey's (USGS) "National Map" as well as the various states' GIS databases, which are excellent. The National Oceanographic and Atmospheric Administration (NOAA) and the Bureau of Land Management's GIS data were also very helpful.

Charles Preuss's magnificent maps of the West based on his and others' travels with Charles Frémont were invaluable to my creation of the included maps. Other period mapmakers, Howard Stansbury, John W. Gunnison, T. H. Jefferson, Frederick Egloffstein, G. M. Dodge, and Warren A. Ferris all lent a hand to my efforts through their wonderfully composed maps. The USGS and their comprehensive collection of topographical maps were extremely useful as well in charting Sarah's course. Gregory Franzwa's two-volume set of the emigrant trail maps was also very helpful. Erwin Raisz's map, *Landforms of the United States*, adds value to any geographical work, this one included. Roy D. Tea is undoubtedly "the expert" on the Hastings Cutoff through Utah and Nevada. My conversations with him, as well as the information in his two excellent, short volumes of his maps of the Hastings Cutoff were essential to my understanding of that portion of the route.

Because the political boundaries of the west changed under Sarah's feet as she made her way along the Humboldt River in today's central Nevada, I did not attempt to capture the 1850 political boundaries on the maps. Instead, I found the maps more clear if I simply used the current-day state boundaries. I did, however, attempt to reduce the physical features on the maps to those of 1850. For the most part, this effort involved eliminating over a dozen reservoirs that did not exist in 1850 and depicting specific rivers in their 1850 channels.

As place names change over time, there are likely several names for the same locale. For standardization, I prioritized place names in the following order: the name given by Sarah first, then the name in use (or on the maps) closest to 1850—primarily using the 1848 Preuss map or the 1849 Jefferson map—and then the oldest name given by the USGS Board on Geographic Names. Where there is a significant difference from the current name, I placed the current name in parenthesis adjacent to the name used. I have also included, in parenthesis, some other current-day places on the maps to aid the reader.

My wife, Evangeline, was a constant source of strength throughout the two years I carved out of our lives to study and write *Following Sarah*. For her help in everything, I am forever grateful. Maria Brower's continuing encouragement, thoughts, and advice are greatly appreciated. Pat and Jack Fletchers' thoughtful comments, advice, and insights were essential in crafting the final manuscript; I offer my sincere thanks to them. I am extremely grateful to the author and trail historian, Donald E. Buck, whose tremendous support, maps, advice, analysis, and encouragement were invaluable. Many, many thanks to all the librarians along the way especially Anne Green of the Doris Foley Historical Library in Nevada City; Jon Wuepper of the Cass County, Michigan, Local History Branch Library; and Adrienne Sharpe of the Beinecke Rare Book and Manuscript Library.

A journey from Michigan to California in 1849 by a young woman and her family represents far more than mere grappling with geography; it represents an abandonment of a previous life and a leap into a complete unknown to start another. Sarah knew that once removed from her world in Young's Prairie, there was little chance she would ever see her parents, family, and friends again. Moreover, there was no guarantee of gold, riches, or even a better life at the other end of the journey. The journey did guarantee hard work and peril. Sarah suffered months of tending for small children in the open expanses of the West, mending, cleaning, freezing temperatures, lightning strikes, wolves, crossing waterless deserts and perilous rivers, encountering aggressive natives, the death of a family member, and bumping through monotonous and endless clouds of dust. Through it all, with the exception of three dour entries, her diary maintained an optimistic tone.

There was no "do-over" and there was no going back. Sarah, her family, and the thousands of other westward travelers of gold rush years were utterly committed to the results of their individual decisions—however good or bad they were. Her experience then is unparalleled today; accordingly, any attempt I make to capture the true essence of her trip falls short—I cannot better Sarah's own words. I can only add some marginal notes to her diary and attempt to shine a light on a map—Sarah did the real work.

Robert Davis
Twentynine Palms, California, 2013

A Note on Locations

While mapping the progress of the Davises' across the continent, I used their evening camping location as a "milepost," assigning a date and placing a dot on a map for each evening's camp. I could have used their noon stop location, or any other point of interest along their path, but I chose their evening location because Sarah fairly consistently described where they stopped and recorded mileages between those evening camps. I've derived these camping locations by comparing Sarah's diary descriptions, dates, and mileages against topographical maps, known trail locations, diaries of other emigrants, guidebooks, terrain, aerial photography, other sources, and the knowledge I gained by attempting to physically follow her route.

Some camp locations were easy to determine. When Sarah comments that they camped at an intersection of a named stream and a river, we can be confident they were very close to the same current-day stream intersection. Yet, even in these "high-confidence" cases, there is still some uncertainty. Many of these streams are "meandering streams," and meandering streams, well, meander, so I'm not "overconfident" with those locations. In other cases, we can generally understand where they spent the night based on Sarah's descriptions alone. For example, after crossing the crest of the Sierra Nevada, Sarah remarks, "we have got over and found a bottom covered with grass." Here she's describing "Summit Valley" (still covered with grass today), where she and countless others spent the night after crossing the "Donner Summit" passes. Of course, the assurance of this location is predicated on knowing that they spent the previous day on the other side of Donner Summit, along the "Truckee Route," and not along the "Carson Route."

In other cases, where Sarah only provides minimal specific information, such as: "camped on the prairie," I have far less confidence in the accuracy of the location I ascertained. Yet, I still place a dot on the map that represents my best educated guess based on the analysis of all the other information I found. For instance, perhaps the day after "spending the night on the prairie," Sarah camps in a spot I have high confidence in and she provided a total mileage traveled that day. Armed with this, and any other corroborating information (location of streams, known camping locations, etc.), I'm able to backtrack along the trail to a probable camping location for the night before.

xv

I consider Sarah's recorded mileages fairly reliable. Indeed, in most cases, I simply took Sarah at her word when it came to distance traveled. However, those mileages are only one element of the larger set of information; accordingly, differences may arise between Sarah's recorded mileages and the mileages to the camping locations ascertained by that larger body of evidence. In these cases, I've adjusted her recorded mileages with "measured mileages" of my own. Of course, Sarah was there in 1850 when she wrote those mileages down, I was not.

Regardless of how confident I am with the location of any specific camping spot, I am confident with the "fit" of each camping spot between the one before it and the one after it. The understanding of each location depends on the understanding of the previous locations as well as of the following locations. Their route, indeed the essence of their entire journey, is an unbroken chain of moves and events that can only be understood by appreciating it as a whole, from Michigan to California, and not any single day's events.

A Note about Forks in the Road

There were several forks in the trail encountered by emigrants in 1850. Unless Sarah specifically stated which fork they took, I simply attempted to follow her mileages and descriptions along each fork until information confirmed one and denied the other. For instance, in the case of Scotts Bluff, where there were two common routes, this information presents itself quickly: Sarah's description of a trading post occupied by French men, native women, and a blacksmith shop can only be Robidoux Trading Post along the southern route. At other times, the differentiating information is not as readily forthcoming. In these cases, I present a differential analysis and conclusions in the text.

A Note on Sarah's Spelling

Sarah's spelling is often phonetic. I've made every effort to transcribe her diary as closely to the original as possible, correcting spelling only when absolutely necessary for clarity.

A Note on Photographs and Maps

All of the photographs (with the exception of the portraits of

Sarah and Zeno in chapters one and six) were taken by the author at or very close to the latitudes and longitudes indicated in their respective captions. The included maps, unless otherwise indicated, were created by the author.

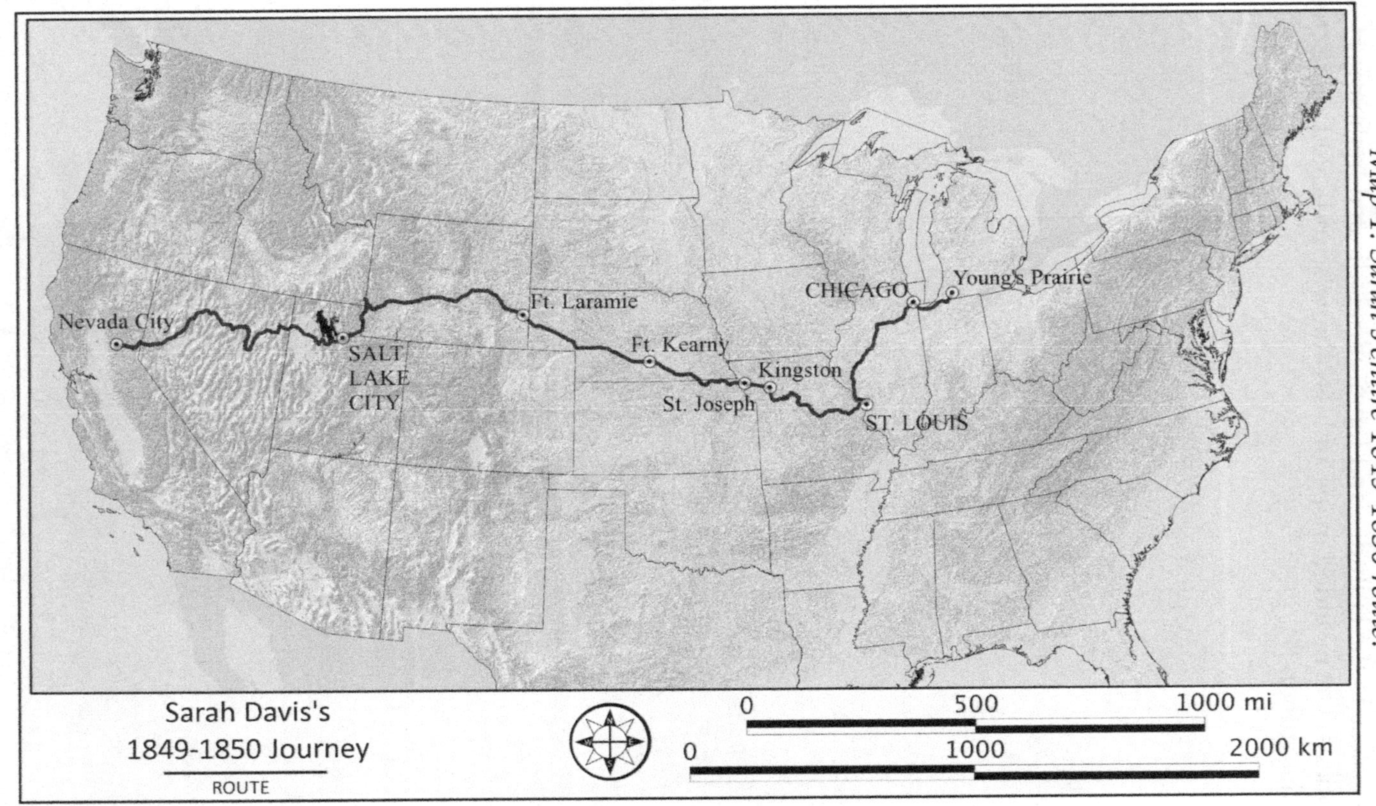

Map 1. Sarah's entire 1849-1850 route.

Chapter One
Introduction

Started for Califarnia march 5th 1849 Landed April 3rd at St Joseph Mo Same year has wife living in youngs prairie Cass Co Michigan also has on hundred and fifteen dollars in Gold on his person has 2 Brothers Living in Kingston Caldwell Co Mo

Zeno Philosopher Davis, March 1849[1]

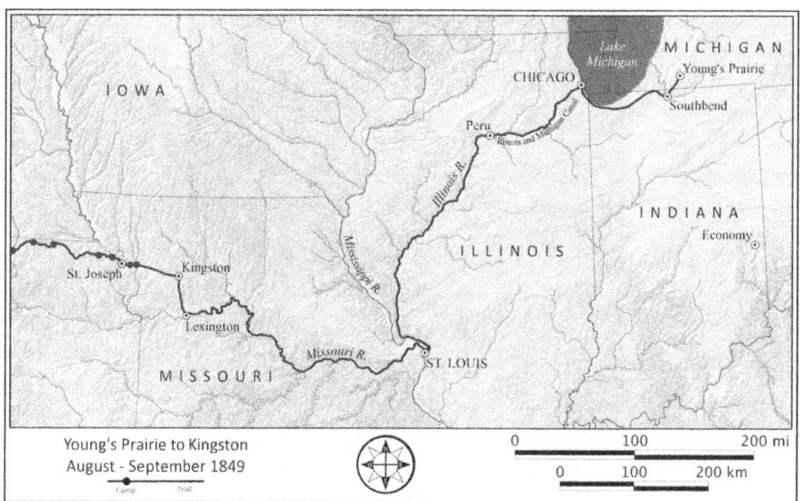

Map 2. The Davises' route between Young's Prairie and Kingston.

In late August 1849, twenty-three-year-old Sarah Davis and her three-week-old daughter, Cleora, left their home in Cass County, Michigan, and headed west.[2] She and her family were part of the great pulse of American emigrants seeking wealth, prosperity, and a better life at the western end of the American continent.

Sarah likely traveled by rail or stage to Chicago, then followed the Illinois and Michigan Canal to Peru, Illinois, where they embarked on a riverboat and followed the Illinois River to St. Louis. From St. Louis, they took another riverboat up the Missouri River to Lexington, Missouri.[3] Sarah and Cleora were accompanied by Sarah's thirty-four–year-old brother-in-law, Alexander Davis.[4]

On the afternoon of 5 September 1849, after almost 600 miles traveling, Sarah, Cleora, and Alexander descended the ramp of a riverboat onto the shore of Lexington. Waiting for them was the tall, gray-eyed Zeno Philosopher Davis, Sarah's husband, who had traveled to the St. Joseph area previously.[5]

Zeno and Sarah had married on the Fourth of July, 1844, when Sarah was eighteen, in a family friend's home in Cassopolis, Michigan.[6] Five years later, on 9 August 1849, she gave birth to her first child, Cleora Adelaide.[7]

Figure 1. Sarah Davis in 1879. (From the author's private collection.)

Within a few days after arriving in Lexington, Sarah, Zeno, Cleora, and Alexander traveled by road for the two-day trip to Kingston, Missouri. Kingston was (and is) a small farming community located about forty-five miles east of St. Joseph, Missouri. Waiting in Kingston were twenty-six-year-old Edwin Davis, Zeno's younger brother, and Sarah Ann, the wife of either Alexander or Edwin, more probably Alexander.[8] Sarah Ann had an infant child, whose name is not recorded.

Kingston, however, was not the party's ultimate goal; it was a jumping off point for their covered wagon journey to California, where "gold in quantities beyond computation" was discovered the previous year.[9]

Zeno had tried to reach California alone in 1849. Leaving a pregnant Sarah in Young's Prairie, he traveled from Michigan to St. Joseph in early March after signing on with the "Pawpaw Mining Company of Michigan."[10] Perhaps due to a cholera outbreak, Zeno never ventured past St. Joseph.[11] Instead, it seems he took up residence with his two brothers and Sarah Ann in nearby Kingston.[12] There, he probably worked as a gunsmith and blacksmith, trades he learned from his father.[13]

Figure 2. Zeno Davis in 1879. (From
the author's private collection.)

In Kingston, the Davises undoubtedly assembled wagons, cattle, and the equipment required for a trip planned for the spring of 1850.[14] Once assembled, their covered wagon outfit probably consisted of at least two wagons, twenty or twenty-five heads of cattle, and three or four horses. The wagons were loaded with about 500 pounds of food per person, casks for water, firearms, tools, clothing, and household items.[15]

While they had a start point, Young's Prairie, and an overland trail jumping off point, Kingston, there remains some question as to where they were going. It appears that Sarah may have thought they were going to Oregon. Two months after leaving Kingston, in July, Sarah makes her only comment concerning their destination: "I think...

we go to oregon...." This singular comment should be balanced against a larger body of evidence suggesting their destination was California.

In 1849, when Zeno set out alone, his first journal entry, "...Started for Califarnia march 5th 1849," specifies that California was at least *his* destination. Also, Zeno's signing on with a mining company clearly indicates that gold, or its economic derivatives, was his objective. Moreover, when Sarah and Zeno traveled west in 1850, their actions, decisions, and routes never committed them to Oregon. When Sarah wrote her Oregon entry, they had just embarked on Sublette's Cutoff, a trail leading either to Oregon or California; the geographic point that demanded a choice between the two was still over two hundred miles distant in current-day Idaho—a point that they would never reach, for they turned south after reaching the Bear River to join the Hastings Cutoff route, a trail leading through Salt Lake City and then to California.[16] Nevertheless, when Sarah wrote the diary entry, she seemed confident they were traveling to Oregon. Perhaps they were headed to Oregon but changed their minds, or perhaps they had not decided; whichever the case, the inertia of Zeno's earlier effort to reach California and their decisions along the way propelled them to California.

On the nineteenth of May, 1850, the "Davis Party," Sarah, Zeno, Cleora, Alexander, Edwin, Sarah Ann, and Sarah Ann's child, left Kingston by covered wagon for California. For the next 152 days and 1,972 miles, Sarah and her family would follow a collection of emigrant trails through current-day Missouri, Kansas, Nebraska, Wyoming, Utah, Nevada, and California. They crossed the Great Plains, the Rocky Mountains, the Wasatch Range, the Great Salt Desert, the Ruby Mountains, the "Forty-Mile Desert," and the Sierra Nevada before arriving in Nevada City on 17 October 1850.

On the twenty-first of May, between Kingston and St. Joseph, while camped along the Platte River, Sarah Davis started writing in a small notebook about the day's events and her surroundings.[17] Sarah continued writing a day-by-day account of the rest of her journey, filling 115 pages with cursive words from top to bottom and side to side. Rarely does a day's entry take more than one side of one notebook sheet. Sarah wrote in ink or pencil. Though Sarah's spelling and grammar may have suffered, her thoughts are clear and direct—she knew what she wanted to say.

Notes

[1] Sarah Davis, "Diary of Sarah Davis" (Yale Collection of Western Americana, Beinecke Rare Book and Manuscript Library, Yale University, 1850), Zeno Philosopher Davis's entry. This first entry of Zeno Philosopher (Z. P.) Davis (Sarah Davis's husband) establishes the date he left Cass County, Michigan, and the date he arrived in St. Joseph. He is careful to establish his family and possessions, presumably in case something ill should happen to him. The first few pages of the notebook containing Sarah's diary are filled with Zeno's notes.

[2] William W. Hinshaw, *Encyclopedia of American Quaker Genealogy* (Baltimore: Genealogical Pub. Co, 1969), V:840; Alfred Mathews, *History of Cass County, Michigan: With Illustrations and Biographical Sketches of Some of Its Prominent Men and Pioneers* (Chicago, IL: Waterman, Watkins & Co., 1882; reprint, Evansville, IN: Unigraphic, Inc., 1971; reprint, Lansing, MI: Inter-Collegiate Press Service Center, 1985), 247. Sarah was born in Preble County, Ohio, on 1 May 1826. She was the seventh of Sarah Jones and Amos Green's eleven children. In 1830, when Sarah was four years old, she moved with her family to Cass County, where they settled in an area known as Young's Prairie.

[3] Seymour Dunbar, *History of Travel in America,* New ed. (New York: Tudor, 1937), 1096. This is a description of the general route that was taken, not a specific account of the Davises' journey.

[4] Minerva Lester Power, "Letter to Mr. Davis," October 8, 1851, Searls Library, Nevada City, CA. According to Power's recollection, Alexander was sent from Kingston to Young's Prairie to escort Sarah and Cleora to Kingston.

[5] Minerva Lester Power, "Davis Family" (unpublished, September 20, 1942), 5; Cleora Lester (Davis), "Pioneer of 1850 Tells of Her Coming to California," The Morning Union (Nevada City, CA, October 21, 1924); Davis, "Diary of Sarah Davis," Z. P. Davis entry of 5 September 1849; "Great Register of Nevada County," 1892, Doris Foley Historical Library, Nevada City, CA. According to his granddaughter, Minerva Power, Zeno Philosopher Davis was born on 22 June 1818. The evidence for the Lexington shore meeting is a synthesis of Cleora's assertion that she was only three weeks old when she and her mother left Michigan, and Zeno's notes that have him traveling to Lexington to meet a boat on 5 September 1849. The Great Register establishes Zeno's height and eye color.

[6] "Cass County Marriages, Liber B," n.d., Cass District Library, Local History Branch, Genealogy and Research, Cassopolis, MI, entry for Zeno P. Davis and Sarah Green recorded 1 July 1844. The family friend is J. Barnum, probably Joshua Barnum.

[7] Power, "Davis Family," 5.

[8] Sarah Davis, "Diary of Sarah Davis as Transcribed by Minerva L. Power," ed. Minerva Lester Power, ca. 1940. Notes by Minerva Power, Sarah's granddaughter, establish Sarah Ann as Sarah's sister-in-law. However, the record is silent on whether Sarah Ann is Edwin's or Alexander's wife. Circumstantial evidence points to Alexander as the husband: Alexander traveled with a wagon. In Sarah Davis's diary, there is never any mention of Edwin having a wagon, though there is considerable mention of Alexander's wagon (which had a tendency of falling over). Based on this, it seems likely the brother with the wagon was also the brother with the wife and child. However, Sarah not mentioning a wagon for Edwin does not exclude the possibility he had one and, therefore, does not exclude him from being the husband.

[9] Dunbar, 1270.

[10] Davis, "Diary of Sarah Davis," Z. P. Davis's first entry; Louis J. Rasmussen, *California Wagon Train Lists* (Colma, CA: San Francisco Historic Records, 1994), 15. Paw Paw, Michigan, is about twenty-five miles north of Young's Prairie; David Lavender, *The Overland Migrations: Settlers to Oregon, California, and Utah* (Washington, DC: US Department of the Interior, 1980), 73, 77. Zeno's departure date is established in the first entry in Sarah's diary (Zeno used the notebook for notes before Sarah used it as a diary). Zeno may have planned to travel to California without his family in order to establish himself first and then send for his family, or he may have thought to work the California gold mines, either as a smith or a miner, then return (presumably a rich man) to Young's Prairie and his family, as was a common plan for male emigrants in 1849.

[11] Hubert H. Bancroft, *History of California* (San Francisco, CA: The History Company, 1890), VI:149; Power, "Letter to Mr. Davis;" Lester (Davis), "Pioneer of 1850 Tells of Her Coming to California," 4; Lawrence P. Shelton, *California Gunsmiths 1846-1900* (Fair Oaks, CA: Far West Publishers, 1977), 80. In a 1924 speech given by Cleora later in life, she recalled that her family spent the winter of 1849-1850 in St. Joseph. Alternatively, Shelton places Zeno, alone, in St. Louis during this same winter. However, other evidence suggests it is more likely the Davises spent that winter in Kingston. As mentioned, Zeno had family in Kingston, so it is reasonable to assume that following his March 1849 decision not to travel past St. Joseph, Zeno stayed with his brothers in nearby Kingston. Also in September, when Sarah traveled to join Zeno, she landed at Lexington, not St. Joseph and not St. Louis. Lexington is the nearest Missouri River port to Kingston. Furthermore, when Zeno traveled to meet Sarah in Lexington, he logged his progress (in the same notebook which would later contain Sarah's diary) along a path

between Kingston and Lexington ("Started from Kingston first vilage [sic] Knoxville fourteen miles Richmond 14 miles Lexington 12 mi..."). Lastly, Sarah's first diary entry written in late May, as she was traveling west, places her a day's travel east of St. Joseph, between Kingston and St. Joseph. Therefore, while neither Sarah nor Zeno explicitly state that they spent the winter in Kingston, Zeno's family there, Sarah's arrival port, Zeno's travel log, and Sarah's early diary entry all suggest they did.

[12] Davis, "Diary of Sarah Davis," 5 March 1849 entry. The question remains as to who these brothers were. Zeno had five brothers: Alexander, Allen W., Alfred, Edwin, and Elihu. Of these, the 1850 US Census has Elihu living in Gratis, Ohio, and Allen living in Cass County, Michigan. This leaves Alexander, Alfred, and Edwin as possible Kingston residents. We know that Alexander and Edwin are the two brothers who joined Zeno and Sarah for the cross-country trip, so it is likely (but not definite-Alexander may well have lived in Cass County, traveled with Sarah to Kingston, and then he and Edwin made the trip with Sarah and Zeno) those are the two who lived in Kingston.

[13] "United States Census, 1850," index and images, FamilySearch (https://familysearch.org/pal:/MM9.1.1/MHV6-Q6H : accessed 6 June 2012), Elihu Davis in household of Elihu Davis, Economy, Wayne, Indiana, United States. This 1850 Census lists Elihu's occupation as a blacksmith.

[14] Joseph E. Ware, *The Emigrant's Guide to California* (St. Louis, MO: Union Office, 1849; reprint, New Jersey: Princeton University Press, 1932; reprint, New York, NY: De Capo Press, 1972), 3n4. The Davises used Kingston as a staging area to prepare for the overland trip. Zeno and his brothers built their wagon outfits there, avoiding having to haul equipment and livestock from Michigan as well as the expense of building their outfit through high-priced outfitters in St. Joseph. Kingston allowed them the time and space to assemble and prepare for the trip on their terms.

[15] Ibid., 5–6.

[16] US National Park Service, *California National Historic Trails Comprehensive Management and Use Plan: Final Environmental Impact Statement* (United States Department of the Interior, 1998), 38.

[17] This is the Platte River just east of St. Joseph, which runs from northern Missouri and meets the Missouri River across from Leavenworth, Kansas, not the Platte River flowing through Nebraska.

Chapter Two
The Great Plains

*when I went to Sarah she was no beter and I soon saw
she would die and she did die before noon   o how lonely I felt to think I was all the woman in company and
too s[m]all babies left in my care it seams to me as if I
would be hapy if I only had one woman with me*

Sarah Davis, 24 June 1850

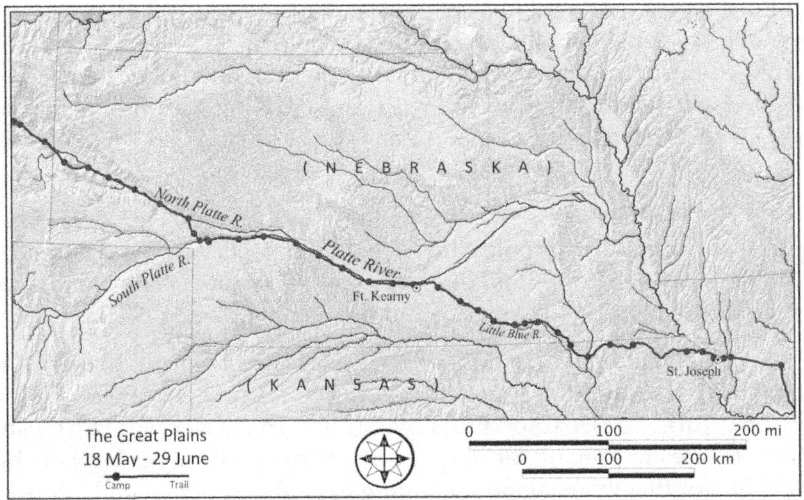

Map 3. The Great Plains.

It took the Davises forty days to cross the Great Plains and reach Fort Laramie in present-day Wyoming. After passing through St. Joseph, they headed west across Kansas then followed the Little Blue River northwest until 9 June when they struck a more northerly direction for Fort Kearny, Nebraska. From Fort Kearny, they traveled along the south side of the Platte River for about 150 miles, keeping along the South Platte where the river forked. The Davises followed the trail northwest as it crossed the South Platte and then continued over the peninsula separating the South and North Platte Rivers. They arrived at Ash Hollow on 23 June. From Ash Hollow, they followed the south bank of the North Platte River to Fort Laramie passing Courthouse Rock, Chimney Rock, and Scotts Bluff. They arrived at Fort Laramie on 30 June.

Sarah Ann, Sarah Davis's sister-in-law, died just past Ash Hollow. Sarah Davis mentions that Sarah Ann fell ill, presumably from cholera, on 23 June in Ash Hollow. Sarah Ann was dead before noon the next day. Sarah Ann was buried either at the noon location (vicinity of current-day Oshkosh, Nebraska) or at their Rush Creek camping spot on the twenty-fourth.

*   *   *

Tuesday, 21 May 1850 (the nineteenth, twentieth, and twenty-first were spent traveling between Kingston and the Platte River).

The diary of Sarah Davis begins:

> *mrs. Z P Davis 1850*
> *May 21 we camped on the Plat river and also lost our cattle I have bin viewing the plat river and I think it is beautifull so I think I will write a little on the subject   their is plenty of birds to warble their beautiful notes and some beautiful ducks and their young are accasionaly seen and a few geese I saw a snake that some one had killed that was five feet long and as large as l [unreadable]*

Sarah's group stopped for the night along the Platte River (Missouri's Platte river, running south from around Des Moines, Iowa and meeting the Missouri River across from Leavenworth, Kansas) thirty-eight miles west of Kingston, Missouri. Neither Sarah nor Zeno kept any record of their trip from Kingston to the Platte.

Wednesday, 22 May 1850.

> *may 22 we camped on the black snake hills[1] in bucanan county in one mile of St Joseph and a pleasenter place I never saw the beautifull building I never saw the like and the droves of Catle and mules and the prairie hens beautiful tongue canot tell the after rale [...after all..?] of the beautiful green as fair as the eye can see   a more beautiful sight I never saw*

The party traveled about seven miles to position themselves in the hills about a mile east of the Missouri River and St. Joseph.

Thursday, 23 May 1850.

may 23 we traveled through st joseph and then through the missouri bottom

Since Sarah doesn't mention crossing the Missouri River and since there did not seem to be any delay, they apparently crossed the river without incident. Wagon trains would line up along the streets of St. Joseph waiting their turn to ferry across, and sometimes there were delays.[2] Once across, the Davises camped near current-day Wathena, Kansas, which is on the bluffs six miles from St. Joseph.

Figure 3. Missouri River ferry site at the foot of Francis Street in St. Joseph. (Camera location: 39.7667°N 94.8609°W facing north.)

Friday, 24 May 1850.

> *may 24 we camped* [on 23 May] *on the bluffs 6 miles from st joseph and staid a half a day and cooked and wasde and then started on and then we had a vary bad time with the Indians one of them was drunk and he ordered us of the land and we told him we would not go and he then got down from his pony and said we should we also told him if he did not go home we would whip him and then he got In arage and said whip whip whip god dam you puchall puchall and wanted us to leave and he then wanted some money just one picaune and quarter of a dollar and then Edwin told him to leave again and he would not and then they led his pony to the road and then he left we also parted with* [? unreadable] *Houston that* [? unreadable] *us to the plains this morning one of the best fellows in the world I believe*

The Davises traveled less than a half a mile on the twenty-fourth, a tentative traveling day. The drunken native would have slowed them somewhat, but the longer delay was probably caused by the friction involved with organizing into a "company" of fellow emigrants.

Minerva L. Power, Sarah and Zeno's granddaughter, and the first to transcribe Sarah's diary (adding notes of clarification and interest based on conversations with her grandparents), writes that her grandfather, Zeno, was elected the captain of a train of "forty wagons," but he turned down the position after Sarah vigorously objected.[3] Though Sarah's diary contradicts the size of the train, describing its size as five or six wagons, it is evident that they fell in with a company of fellow emigrants, as the following day's entry makes clear.

Saturday, 25 May 1850.

> *may 25 we camped* [on 24 May] *on the plains a half amile from the place we at befor with five or six wagons in company the next day* [today, 25 May] *we started in and traveled fourteen miles to musketo ceek* [creek] *and then we had a plesent time for we got in company with a mr Right a cosin of Sarah ann and he had ten wagons and fifty men*

The Davises camped along the trail at Mosquito Creek, about three miles north of today's Troy, Kansas.

Sunday, 26 May 1850.

may 26 we traveled all day and past the Indians station of five or six houses and one store and a large farm and then we camp on the planes near a small creek whare they say there is no wood nor water for thirty miles

The Davises camped at Cedar Creek, fourteen miles west of their Mosquito Creek camp and just west of Samuel Irvin's Presbyterian mission. Irvin's mission, established to teach the Iowa, Fox, and Sac Indians, is likely the structures Sarah mentions in her diary.[4] According to a plaque at the mission's location, the original mission was constructed in 1845 and was "originally 106 feet long contained 32 rooms, including a dining hall and chapel."

may 26 we crost wolf river

This entry appears after the 27 May entry and looks like an afterthought. The Wolf River is east of Irvin's mission. The Davises crossed over the Wolf River early on 26 May.

Monday, 27 May 1850.

may 27

Sarah only records the date.

Tuesday, 28 May 1850.

No entry.

Wednesday, 29 May 1850.

may 29 we crost nimaha river and camped on a creek

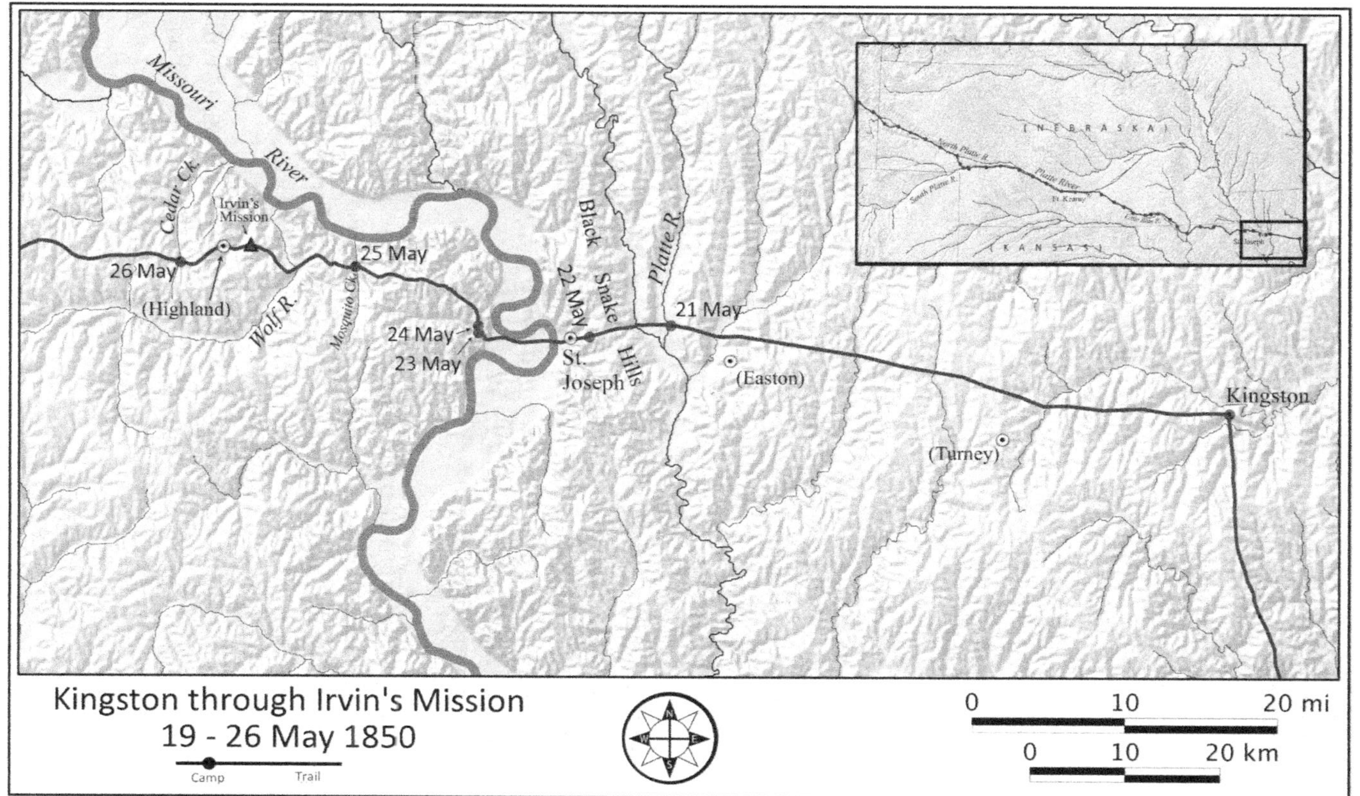

Map 4. Kingston through Irvin's mission.

The Davises spent this night just to the west of the south fork of the Nemaha River, probably along a tributary, current-day Turkey Creek.

Thursday, 30 May 1850.

may 30 we crost creek whare their had bin a man robed and suposd to {have bin} [inserted above] killed it is about one hundred miles from st joseph there is some butifull timber their I think on the river we stoped on the plains to take diner whare there is no wood no water no birds of any kind to be seen   it is prarie as far as the eye can see

After traveling just over nineteen miles, the Davises camped along the trail near Robidoux Creek (south of today's Summerfield, Kansas). The timber seen was along the Clear Creek swale, about halfway through the day's trek.[5]

Friday, 31 May 1850.

may 31 we crost the blue river whare their was a man droned and one died and to turned back to go home we left our company and joined a nother company and we all went a half mile from the river and then camped for the night   we then started on the next morning and traveled till noon and then we stoped for the night

After traveling just over twenty miles, the Davises crossed the Blue River at present-day Marysville, Kansas, and then camped for the night. They either crossed using a ferry that was established in 1850 or at a low-water ford close to where today's Highway 36 crosses the river.[6]

Just west of Marysville, their trail merged with the Independence Road coming from the southwest. Past this intersection was probably where they joined the other company Sarah mentions.

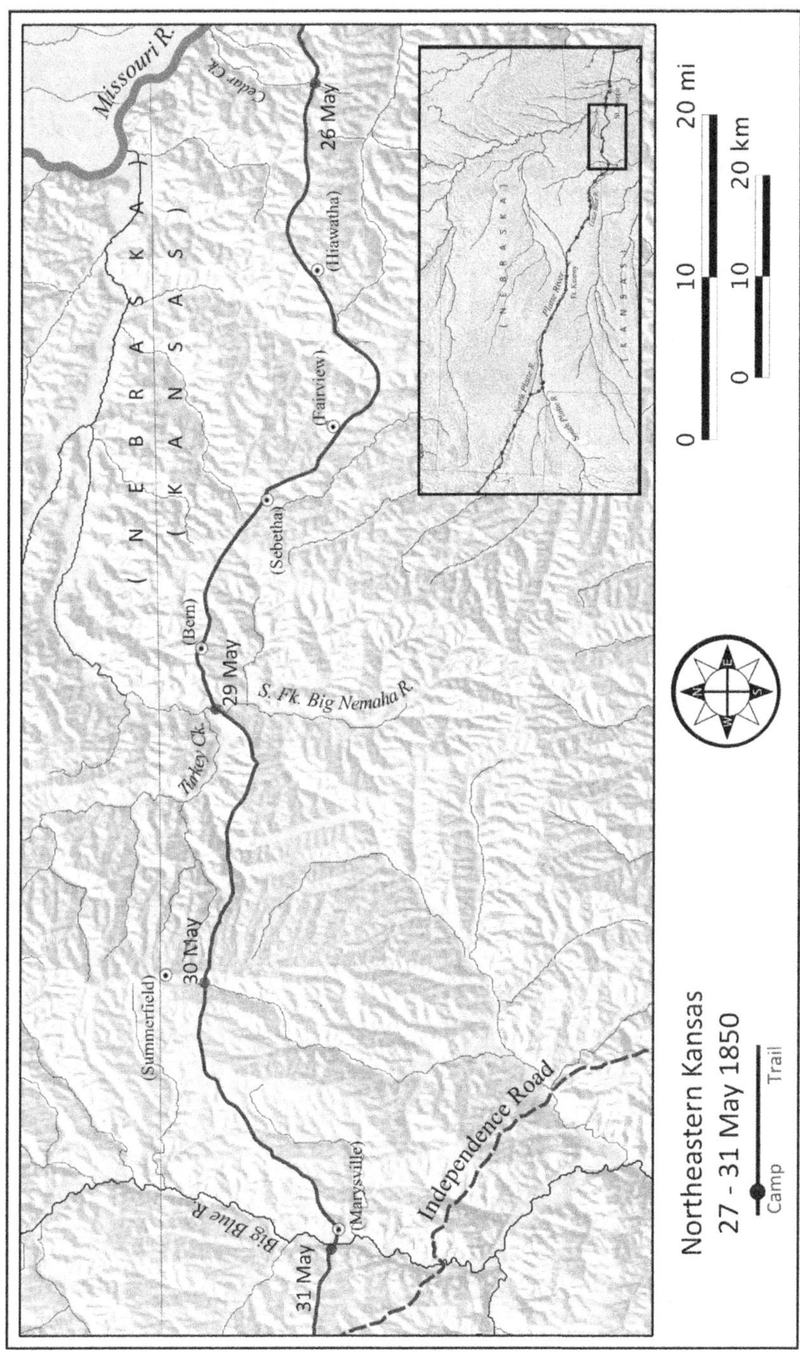

Map 5. Northeastern Kansas.

Saturday, 1 June 1850.

> *june 1 we crost the* [q?]*uiet creek* [probably today's Cottonwood Creek, just west of Hanover, Kansas] *and then we past nine graves that day and past trough plesents prarie as we have past at all I think*

They spent this night along a tributary to the Little Blue River, about seventeen miles from the previous-day's camping spot. Here, they were just two miles south of the current-day border between Nebraska and Kansas.

Sunday, 2 June 1850.

> *june 2 we camped on the prarie a vary plesent place*

Fourteen miles from their 1 June camping location put the Davises astride Rock Creek, where they camped for the evening. In 1858, Rock Creek Station was opened here to serve emigrants and the Pony Express. The Nebraska State Park Service currently maintains the station.

Monday, 3 June 1850.

> *june 3 we crost the big sandy and then had a tremenduous thunder souer it raind till every thing was wet as they could be and still continue to rain till next day*

They spent a wet night just on the west side of the Big Sandy Creek (a tributary of the Blue River) along the Oregon Trail, about three miles west of current-day Powell, Nebraska.

Tuesday, 4 June 1850.

> *june 4 we started on the next morning a and it still continued to rain   and traveled on for eight miles and then camped for the night*

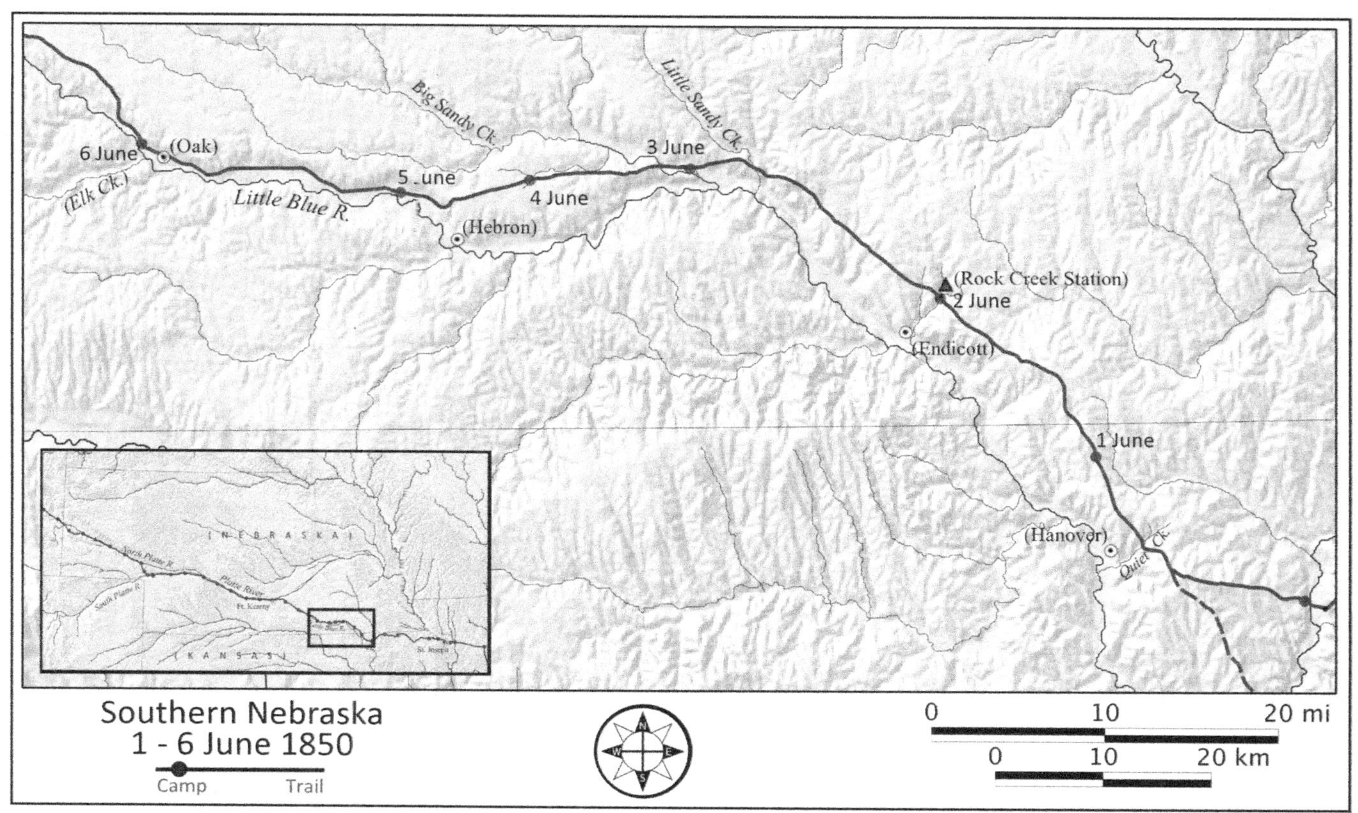

Map 6. Southern Nebraska.

Slogging along a wet, muddy trail, the Davises only made eight miles before camping on the prairie northeast of current-day Hebron, Nebraska.

Wednesday, 5 June 1850.

june 5 we staid on the little blue for one day and washed and dried our close and baked bread and then the next morning we start on

Another wet day brought the Davises to the northern bank of the Little Blue River after eight miles of travel.

Thursday, 6 June 1850.

june 6 we traveled on for the day and nothing hapened of any importance

Traveling sixteen miles, the Davises stopped for the night northwest of current-day Oak, Nebraska. They camped along the Little Blue River.

Friday, 7 June 1850.

june 7 we camped on the blue and I saw one of the largest wolfs I evere saw in my life it was a gray wolf

After fourteen miles, the Davises remained along the banks of the Little Blue River. They camped on the opposite bank from current-day Deweese, Nebraska. This first encounter with wolves would not be the last.

Saturday, 8 June 1850.

june 5 [8] we camped on the little blue and had a tremendous thunder shouer in the evening I saw six antelope that day and one buffalo

More rain and fifteen miles brought them to the north bluff above the Little Blue River, astride Pawnee Creek.

Sunday, 9 June 1850.

> *june 9 camped on plains in the a butiful place whare their was about fifty wagons in camp and then we left the blue river and came in sight of nebraiska* [Platte River[7]]

Peeling off of the Little Blue River just after starting, the Davises continued along the Nebraska plains until they were just west of current-day Kenesaw, Nebraska, where they spent the night on the prairie.

Monday, 10 June 1850.

> *june 10 we stoped to noon and let the catle feed and then to of our men got mad and went on one was one was captain reed and the other was mr donnal we told them to find a good campen* [unreadable] *and a gain we came on that evning but seing that they would not join then they decided to come back to the company that evening so we all camped for the night we traveled eighteen miles that day I saw one sand lizard that day we parted at fort carney three hundred and twenty five miles and it seems good to see a house a gain*

After twenty-three days and over three-hundred miles, the Davis party arrived at Fort Kearny, Nebraska. Sarah's comment about "parting" probably means they left the company of the Reed party. This day they traveled almost twenty miles, and then spent the night near the fort. (The Army was not allowing anyone to camp closer than one mile to the fort.)[8]

Tuesday, 11 June 1850.

> *june 11 we left fort carney and traveled on   we traveled on the bottom of the river   at fort carnney thare was some men in company that sold lquor to the soldiers and they were fiend and to of them taken to the forte and confined and the rest of their liquor turned out of the casque*

They camped fifteen miles west of the fort by a small stream.

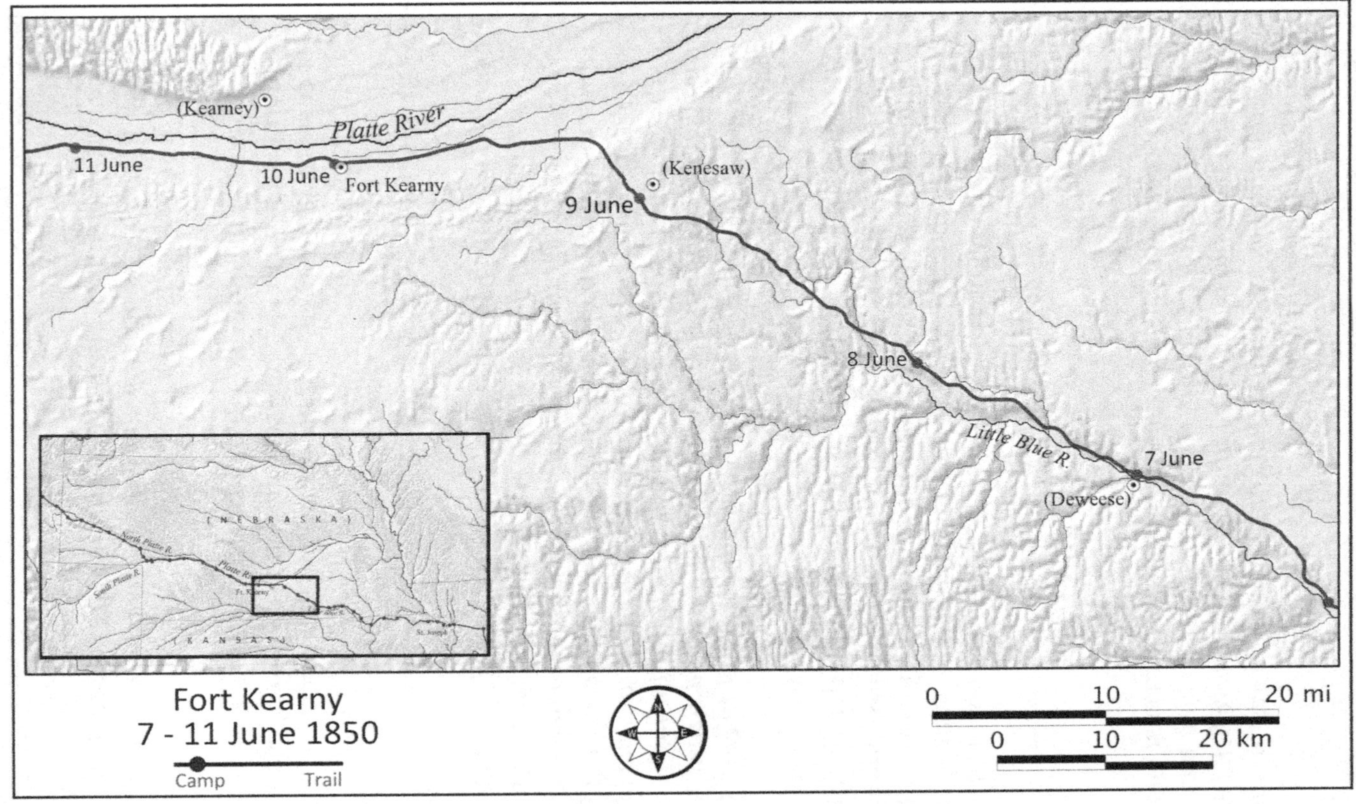

Map 7. Fort Kearny.

Wednesday, 12 June 1850.

> *june 12 we come in company with the cincinatte train and [joined?] with them   we traveled about ten miles   I also saw a butiful flour that Sarah found   it seamed to be a spiecia of prickley pare   the flour was beautiful as I eversaw   I also saw prickley pare   they grow plenty here   we are now twenty six miles from the forte and en camped on the plum creek one mile from wood or water   the musketeos were so bad they had like to eat us up*[9]

Eighteen miles farther placed the Davises at Plum Creek, a tributary to the Platte River.

Thursday, 13 June 1850.

> *june 13   we nooned on the nebriska whare we had plenty of water   we traveled on eighteen miles that day and camped on the Plat river   I saw twelve graves to day   it semes like a grave yard almost to me   I think we travel on vary well   we traveled a bout ten miles farther   we past thirteen graves*

The Cincinnati Company had a long stride. On this day, and each of the next several days, the Davises moved at about twenty miles per day. They spent this night along the Platte across the river from current-day Cozad, Nebraska.

Friday, 14 June 1850.

> *june 14   we travel right in the botom of the Plat we have past six graves to day   we past tueve [twelve] more and one grave that they had not put the body in yet   we had a plesent campen ground last night no musetoes at al and plenty of wood*

After a long day, the Davises camped along the Platte, southeast of Brady, Nebraska.

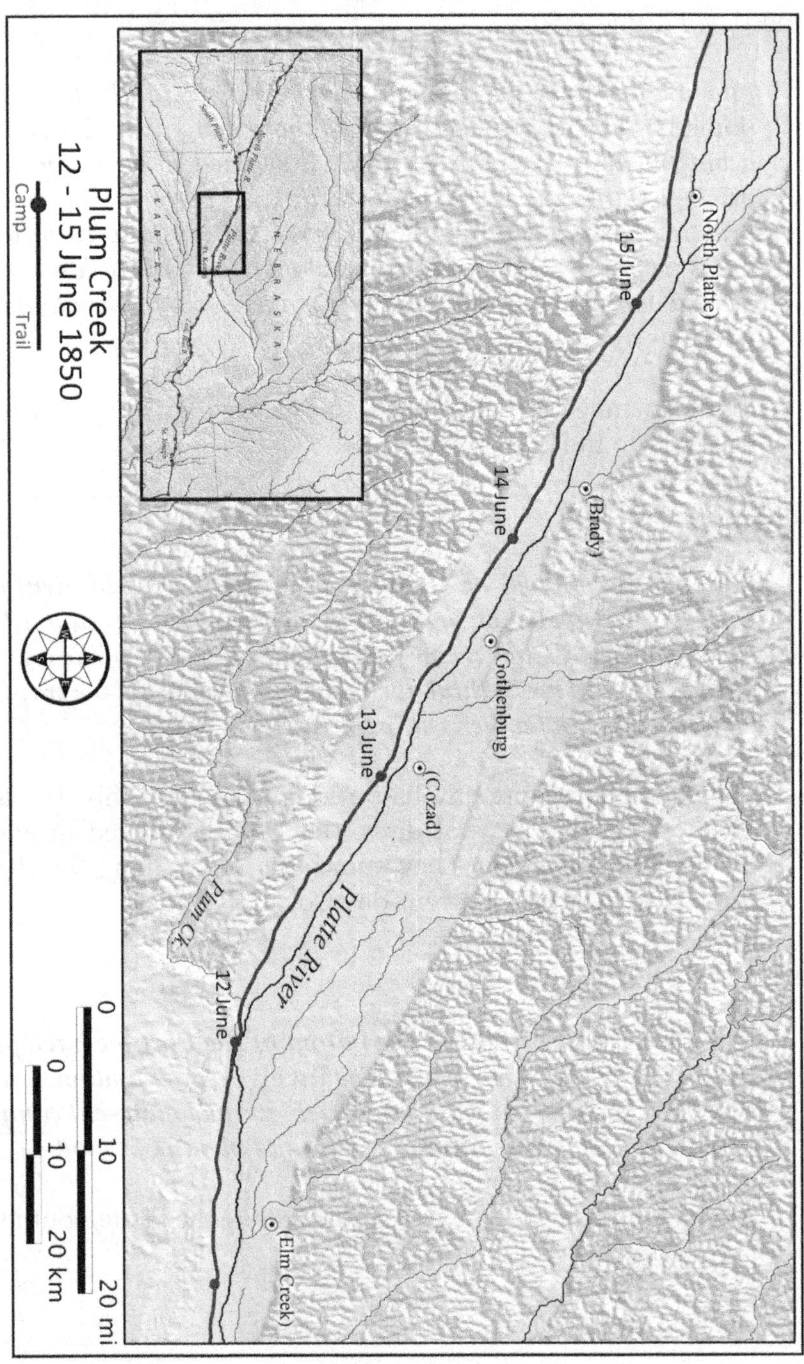

Map 8. Plum Creek.

Saturday, 15 June 1850.

> *june 15 we now have past a long ridge of blufs and come to*
> *ash holler   and now we noon   we past seven graves to day*
> *we camped on the plat after traveling eighteen miles and then*
> *Elick kiled a* [calf?]   *we had a fine super that night and mr*
> *Right come and eat breckfast with us*

The long ridgeline that Sarah mentions are the bluffs paralleling the Platte just to the south of current-day Bignell, Nebraska. While Sarah mentions "Ash Hollow," there is no obvious record of an "Ash Hollow" in this area. There is an Ash Hollow along the trail, but it is still a number of day's travel away. The canyon or hollow Sarah mentions may be the current-day Moran Canyon.

Sunday, 16 June 1850.

> *june 16 sunday we traveled next morning ten miles before noon*
> *and one of our company killed a antelope   and we now have*
> *plenty of fresh meat on hand   we got to a good spring and filled*
> *all of casque cantens full of water of the best kind   we past five*
> *or six wagons agoin back they were home sick besids being sick*
> *for they ware sick*

After ten miles of travel, the party found a "good spring" where they "filled all [their] casque canteens full of water of the best kind." This spring is about a mile past the junction of the North and South Platte Rivers and is marked "Cold Spring" on the Franzwa maps and is likely the same spring that Edwin Bryant, an emigrant diarist and author, described as a "spring of cold pure water."[10] The Davises pressed on another eleven miles before camping for the night.

Monday, 17 June 1850.

> *june 17 monday we started on and traveled ten miles and then*
> *nooned and the men all went in a swimin and I sow and wash*
> *we then started on and traveled seven more miles and got to*

a good spring and then camped for the night a lot of us ware their their was three white wolfs atacked a cow and calf they then surrounded the cow and would have killed her but whilst they ware ex erting their kill a mr crous shot one and he droped down and he thought he was dead but he rose again and run of I saw thirten graves to day

The Davises traveled ten miles to noon, and another seven miles to camp. Seventeen miles from Cold Spring put them near what became known as "O'Fallon's Bluffs."[11] Coincidently, this is the same distance Bryant records from the "Cold Spring" before his party would camp for the evening of 16 June 1846.[12]

Tuesday, 18 June 1850.

june 18 tues we came on and camped on the bluff just above the forde

They camped on the south side of the South Platte River along the bluffs about two miles east of current-day Brule, Nebraska. They traveled about twenty-three miles this day.

Wednesday, 19 June 1850.

june 19 we went on and crost the river it was one mile wide we crost at waddells forde and no one got drouned at all I believe we got a crous and camped on the river

According to Madison Berryman Moorman, another 1850 emigrant and diarist, Waddle's ford (Sarah used "Waddell's") was named after an emigrant company leader who crossed his train "six miles below the old ford."[13] Irene D. Paden, who transcribed and edited Moorman's diary and noted author on the emigrant trails, asserts that this ford would then be two miles east of modern-day Brule, Nebraska.[14]

Moorman's location of Waddell's ford, however, does not square well with the previous or following mileages of Sarah's. Sarah records more miles to the next several camps from this location than there are, and fewer miles from their previous camps to the ford than there are. Because of this, the author questions the veracity of Moorman's assertion that the ford is six miles downstream of the Old California Ford. Sarah's mileages would fit better if the ford were located several miles to the east of where Moorman asserts it is. On the other hand, Sarah may have been off in her distances — long on one side of the ford, short on the other.

Since Sarah doesn't account for all the mileages of some of the immediately adjacent days of her crossing (for instance, she didn't record a mileage traveled on the eighteenth), the author has left the somewhat mysterious Waddell's ford where Moorman and Paden left it, six miles east of the Old California Ford.

Regardless of the ford's location, the Davises crossed the South Platte River without incident, traveled a very short distance, and then camped along the river.

Thursday, 20 June 1850.

june 20 we washed and baked bread and had a tremenduous thunder shouer and I supose their ware ahundred wagons past us   our men saw too bare and one white wolf I believe that is all that past that day

They remained in their 19 June camping spot.

Friday, 21 June 1850.

june 21 we traveld a bout ten miles I believe we camped in the river for the last time   it was the south fork and now we leve it in tirely   we only past three graves in all   I believe I saw too large white wolf

The Davises traveled just under six miles before camping for the night (note that Sarah records ten miles). Here, at the "Old California Crossing" or "upper ford," the trail turns north to climb the "California Hill," which ascends the peninsula separating the North and South Platte Rivers.[15] Below California Hill was the last place they could camp on the South Platte.

Saturday, 22 June 1850.

> *saturday june 22 we started on and traveled ten miles and stoped to noon mr janson and mr meadow had a butifull chase after a wolf this morning they run it down and then shot at it and mist it and mr meadow he broke his gun over it head it fell down and then rose again and it run of and they did not kill it.*

The Davises traveled about seven miles this day. After climbing the California Hill, they camped on the the peninsula between the North and South Platte Rivers.

Sunday, 23 June 1850.

> *june 23 we camped in ash holler fifteen miles from whare we campe before and their was a tremendous thunder souer one role after nother tell it killed a horse that was onley one rod from our wagon that night Sarah was taken sick we had no super*

Ash Hollow was clearly a bad experience for the Davises. The thunderstorms brought lightning, which struck and killed a horse less than twenty feet from Sarah's wagon. More ominous, Sarah Ann began to suffer from an illness, most likely cholera, that would kill her the next day.

Monday, 24 June 1850.

> *june 24 we camped on the north fork of the Plat river and Sarah was vary sick their was one woman died in the camp of the colera and was baried the next morning when I went to Sarah she was no beter and I soon saw she would die and she did die before noon o how lonely I felt to think I was all the woman in company and too s[m]all babies left in my care it seams to me as if I would be hapy if I only had one woman with me*

They camped twenty-five miles past Ash Hollow along the Platte at the intersection of today's Rush Creek. Sarah Ann was probably buried here. On the other hand, since Sarah Ann died

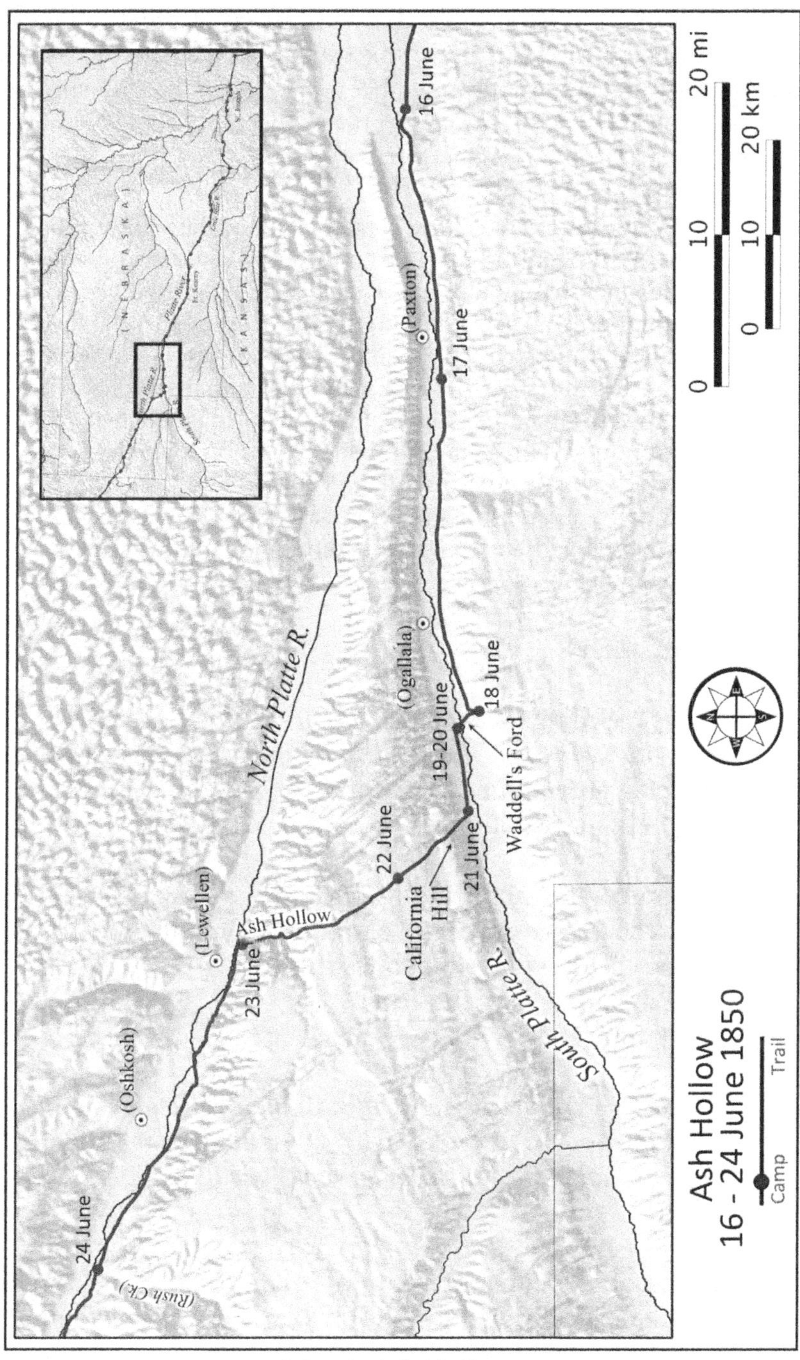

Map 9. Ash Hollow.

before noon, it is possible she was buried at the noon location, just south of current-day Oshkosh, Nebraska. In any case, since this is June, she would have been buried on the day she died.

Minerva L. Power, in her transcription of Sarah's diary recounts Sarah's recollection of the burial of Sarah Ann:

> When the sister-in-law, Sarah, died of the cholera they were obliged to bury her on the plains and a grave was dug and lined with slabs of slate, to keep the wolves from digging it out. The body was then wrapped in a sheet, covered over with slate and the usual fire made on top for the purpose of deceiving the Indians, who often dug up the bodies and scalped them for their belt. My grandmother told me Sarah had beautiful long black hair, which she knew would have been greatly prized by the Indians and many a grave she saw when travelling along, where long hair was trailing out, having been pulled out by the wolves.[16]

Tuesday, 25 June 1850.

> *june 25 we came on and camped on the north plat river within a few rods of fifty sue indians we suposed they ware robers for they had a great many horses of the inglish kind and their was a few french with them*

They spent the night along current-day Deep Holes Creek, across the river and west of today's Broadwater, Nebraska. They traveled twenty-two miles this day.

Wednesday, 26 June 1850.

> *june 26 we coome in sight of chimney rock and nooned buy court house rock it looks like a court house we went on and camped a few miles of chimney rock we had a plesent campen ground*

They nooned along present-day Pumpkin Creek (southeast of current-day Bridgeport, Nebraska) and then made another eleven miles before camping along the Platte, three miles east of Chimney Rock.

Figure 4. Courthouse and Jail Rock as seen from the Emigrant Trail. (Camera location: 41.6215°N 103.0200°W facing south.)

Thursday, 27 June 1850.

thursday june 27 we started on and traveled ten miles and stoped to noon in sight of scots bluffs whare their was plenty of grass for the catle   we traveled twenty miles and encamped in sight of scots bluffs right on the plat river and I washed some that eavning   we had plenty of wolfs to visit us that night they ware all throught the camp

After traveling seventeen miles, they camped along the Platte River, in sight of Scotts Bluff, about five miles east of present-day Gering, Nebraska. The wolves this evening impressed Sarah; she would later recall the night of 27 June to her granddaughter, Minerva:

One night in June, Grandma told me of being surrounded by wolves on the plains near Scotts Bluffs. She said the howling was terrible to hear and on looking out of the wagon as far as she could see were hundreds of firey [sic] eyes in pairs like two red coals, ever drawing nearer as the fire burned lower, she said she fully expected to be eaten alive before morning for she feared the fire would give out, and that was all that kept them off.[17]

Friday, 28 June 1850.

june 28 we nooned near scots buffs and traveled eighteen miles and then crost the bluffs   we crost the bluffs near an Indian vileage   they war siouxe indians and some french men among them   they had a store and a blacksmith s[h]op their ware plenty of them they war expecting a fight evry night from the crow Indians   they insisted on our stain with them that night but we did not like to so we went on three miles and camped

The Indian village with the blacksmith shop is the Robidoux Trading Post (now a National Historic Landmark), operated by the trader of the same name and some of his family members. The post is described as a single log cabin and a cluster of tepees just north of the more southern emigrant trail.[18] Three miles past this post put the Davises along a small wash for the evening.

Figure 5. Chimney Rock as seen from the Emigrant Trail. (Camera location: 41.7155°N 103.3217°W facing south.)

Saturday, 29 June 1850.

june 29 we traveled tuelve miles and stoped to noon   we made a fire and got a cup of tea for diner   I tell you that was good on the planes   we crost too creeks this morning   I saw a mountain

Sheepe horne this morning   it beats all hornes I ever saw   it was five inches through and fifteen Inches long

After traveling twenty-one miles they camped just south of current-day South Torrington, Wyoming. One of the two creeks Sarah mentions is current-day Horse Creek.

Figure 6. Overland trail depression near the site of Robidoux's Trading Post. (Camera location: 41.8030°N 103.8300°W facing southeast.)

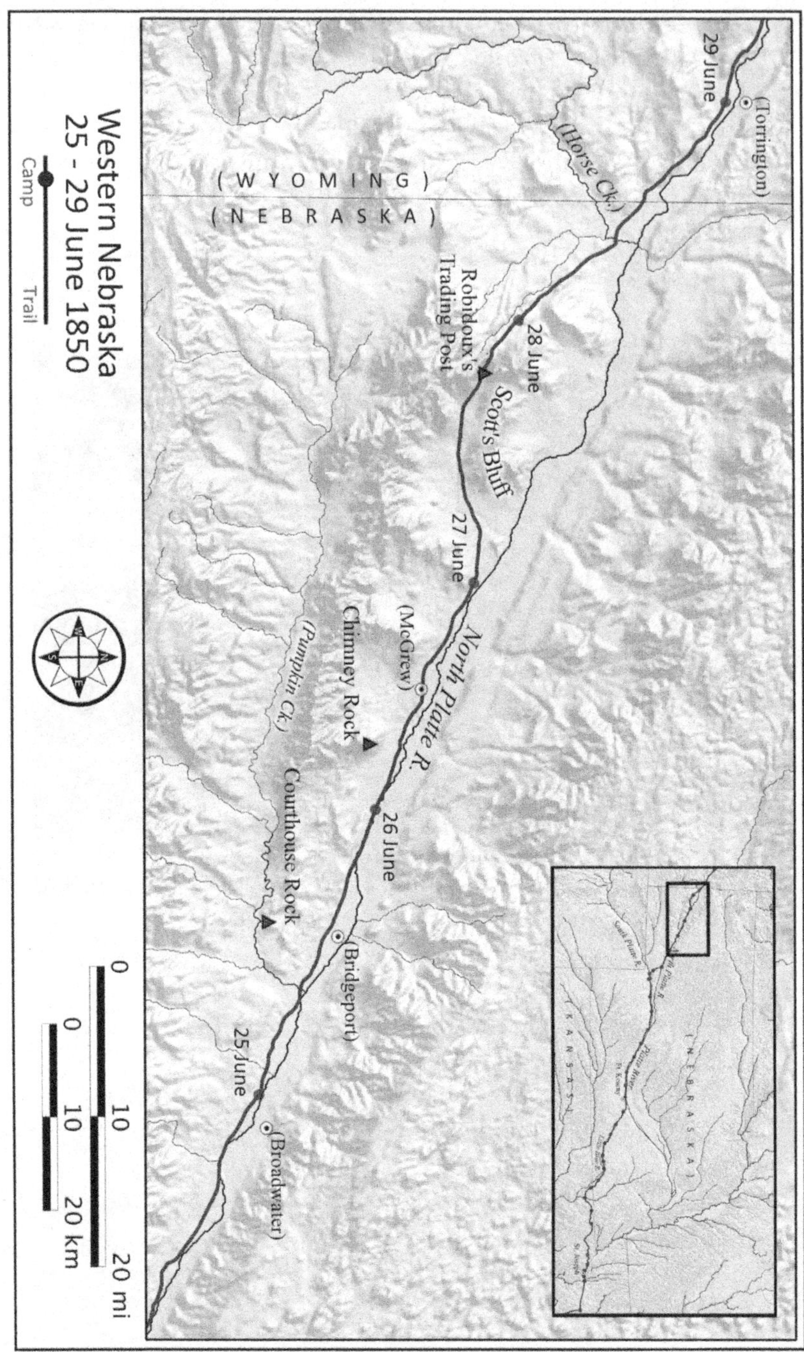

Map 10. Western Nebraska.

Notes

[1] Missouri Immigration Society, *Hand-Book of Missouri* (St. Louis, MO: Times Printing House, 1880), 71. The Black Snake Hills are the hills just to the east of St. Joseph. St. Joseph is situated at the western foot of these hills.

[2] Merrill J. Mattes, *The Great Platte River Road: The Covered Wagon Mainline Via Fort Kearny to Fort Laramie*, 2nd ed. (Lincoln, NE: University of Nebraska Press, 1969), 114.

[3] Sarah Davis, "Diary of Sarah Davis as Transcribed by Minerva L. Power," 1. Minerva formed a close relationship with her grandparents (Sarah and Zeno) while growing up in Nevada City, even spending a year living with them. While transcribing Sarah's diary, Minerva added a preface, titled "Notes pertaining to the Diary." Here, she recorded additional information based on personal conversations with her grandparents. Additionally, Minerva added more notes within the text of the diary.

[4] Frank W. Blackmar, *Kansas: A Cyclopedia of State History, Embracing Events, Institutions, Industries, Counties, Cities, Towns, Prominent Persons, Etc.* (Chicago, IL: Standard Publishing Co., 1912), 1:843, 1:943.

[5] US National Park Service, 248.

[6] John D. Unruh Jr., *The Plains Across: The Overland Emigrants and the Trans-Mississippi West, 1840-60*, 1st unabridged paperback edition, 1993. (Urbana, IL: University of Illinois Press, 1979), 268.

[7] T. H. Jefferson, "Map of the Emigrant Road from Independence Mo. to St. Francisco California," Topographical (New York, NY: T. H. Jefferson, 1849).

[8] Mattes, 203.

[9] Edwin Bryant, *What I Saw in California*, 3rd ed. (New York: D. Appleton & Company, 1849), 81–82. Three passages from Bryant mirror Sarah's descriptions of mosquitoes, ridge lines, and cactus: "The mosquitoes, morning and evening, have been very troublesome since we entered this valley." (10 June), "The bluffs...[have] become more elevated and broken." (11 June), and "I observed the cactus, or common prickley-pear, in bloom, frequently on the march." (11 June).

[10] Gregory Franzwa, *Maps of the California Trail* (Tucson, AZ: Patrice Press, 1999), C17; Bryant, 93.

[11] Franzwa, C18.

[12] Bryant, 94.

[13] Madison Berryman Moorman, *The Journal of Madison Berryman Moorman, 1850-1851* (San Francisco, CA: California Historical Society, 1948), 22.

[14] Ibid, 101n49.

[15] Mattes, xxxii-xxxiii.

[16] Davis, "Diary of Sarah Davis as Transcribed by Minerva L. Power."

[17] Ibid.

[18] Mattes, 440–442.

Chapter Three
The "Rockey" Mountains

we are now in the rockey mountains and it is rockey mountains for certain   t[h]eir is some of the largest rocks I ever saw t[h]eir are some large pine trees here and some cedar tree and plenty of lime stone

Sarah Davis, 4 July 1850

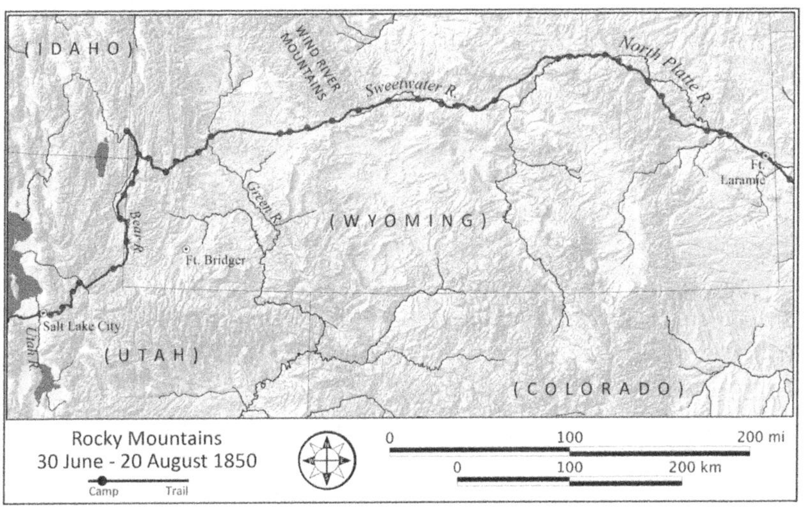

Map 11. The Davises' route across the Rocky Mountains.

Fort Laramie stood as the gateway to the Rocky Mountains. Past the fort, emigrants entered the elevated, dissected, and hilly terrain of the Laramie Range's northern slope, the Black Hills of Wyoming.[1] Within a few days, Sarah saw the vague outline of distant, massive mountain ranges. Within a couple of weeks, she was within those same ranges, following rivers, crossing passes and ridgelines, and struggling through waterless deserts.

After crossing the Laramie River on 30 June, the Davises set up camp near Fort Laramie and then spent a couple of days near the fort. On 2 July, they left the fort and followed the North Platte River to current-day Casper, Wyoming. At this point, the North Platte River comes from the southwest—too south for emigrants heading west to reasonably follow.

Leaving the Platte, they traveled forty-six miles through a waterless desert to reach a tributary of the Sweetwater River near Independence Rock. They continued west along the Sweetwater to the South Pass where, like the Platte before, the Sweetwater ceased its convenient path west. Once through the South Pass, the Davises crossed the Dry Sandy River and then followed its western bank southwest until the trail forked at the "Parting of the Ways"; one fork continuing southwest along the Dry Sandy River and Oregon-California Trail, the other, the Sublette Cutoff, took a more westerly course. Taking the Sublette Cutoff, they made their way across the various branches of the Green River: the Little Sandy, the Big Sandy, the Green itself (crossed by ferry), Fontenelle Creek, and Ham's Fork.

They crossed their second desert of forty-one miles between the Big Sandy and the Green River. Continuing west, they crossed the high, folded ridges of western Wyoming to reach the Bear River valley where they followed the Bear River north until they reached a tributary, Thomas' Fork (in current-day Idaho).[2] At Thomas' Fork, they decided to change course and head to Salt Lake City. After several days of following the Bear River south along today's Utah-Wyoming border, they reached the trail connecting Fort Bridger to Salt Lake City, Hastings Cutoff. Taking Hastings Cutoff west, they traveled over the Wasatch Mountains and arrived in Salt Lake City on 20 August.[3]

The Davises decision to turn south to Salt Lake City after arriving at Thomas' Fork is remarkable. From Thomas' Fork, the more "normal" path to California was to continue northwest along the well-established Oregon-California Trail into southern Idaho, then veer southwest across a corner of Utah into Nevada and to the Humboldt River. Doing so required roughly 350 miles. Turning south to Salt Lake, then across the deserts and around the Ruby Mountains, required 490 miles to reach the same point on the Humboldt. From a mileage and time standpoint, heading to Salt Lake City *after* taking the Sublette Cutoff made little sense.

Nonetheless, there are several possible reasons that could lend logic to their decision. They may have simply followed the wrong trail across western Wyoming — a mistake of navigation. Perhaps they encountered an obstacle preventing them from continuing, or safely continuing, past Thomas' Fork. They may have decided that Salt Lake, a rapidly growing city, could provide the economic base on which they could prosper. They may have needed some part or supply available

38

in Salt Lake City. Maybe there was an unmentioned health concern of one of the travelers. Or, they may have simply changed their minds. We will never know for sure, but we can narrow these possible reasons to a probable.

Figure 7. The hilly, rocky, and forested area just past Fort Laramie. Note the severe ruts (the ditch) in the limestone caused by thousands of wagons on their way west. (Camera location: 42.2560°N 104.7485°W facing west. Photo taken at the Wyoming Oregon (Gurnsey) Ruts and Register Cliff Historic Site.)

Did they intend to travel through Salt Lake on their way to California but mistakenly took the Sublette Trail, only realizing the mistake after arriving at Thomas' Fork?[4] Probably not. Nowhere does Sarah (or Zeno) mention Salt Lake as a waypoint or destination prior to their decision to turn around at Thomas' Fork—nothing suggests that traveling to Salt Lake City was intended prior to the Parting of the Ways. Moreover, they were also quite aware of fellow travelers who split off from their company to travel through Salt Lake to California, as Sarah's entries of 27 and 29 July demonstrate: "we stopped near a train of twenty wagons traders a goin to salt lake" (second 27 July entry) and "I think they went to california and we go to oregon   we parted about noon" (29 July entry). Furthermore, if their destination was Salt

Lake City, and they mistakenly took the Sublette, they would have ferreted out such a mistake along the trail — preparing for and crossing the desert would provide an immediate clue, as would the various river crossings along the Sublette. Had they noticed those clues, it is likely they would not have waited to reach Thomas' Fork to correct the mistake but would have turned south, either at the Big Sandy or once they reached the Bear River, to correct the error. Therefore, traveling the Sublette to Thomas' Fork was an act of commission and not a mistake of navigation.

Was there a requirement for a doctor, or to repair broken equipment, or supplies only available at an established location like Salt Lake City? While a sick or injured member is far from unlikely, Sarah's diary does not mention any. Broken equipment or lack of supplies is also doubtful considering the months the Davises had to prepare and Zeno's blacksmithing skills; again, Sarah is silent on the subject. Furthermore, from Thomas' Fork they were about 100 miles to Fort Hall and 160 miles to Salt Lake City, so, if a town were needed, it was more reasonable to press on to Fort Hall. Therefore, sickness, broken equipment, or lack of critical supplies seem unlikely as probable causes for their turnaround.

Was there some obstacle west of Thomas' Fork, floods, hostile natives, or cholera that compelled them to turn around? If there was, Sarah mentioned none. However, around this time reports surfaced about the poor conditions along the California Trail. In early October (granted, a couple of months distant), Joseph Cain wrote an open letter to the Deseret News describing the difficult conditions he found while returning to Salt Lake City from the gold fields of California. Cain described cholera, significant native problems, and general strife throughout his entire journey (Cain's party returned via the Salt Lake Cutoff).[5] Cain also reported a native "stronghold at the head of Mary's River [Humboldt River]" that the Davises would avoid if they took the Hastings Cutoff through Salt Lake City. Of course, there is nothing suggesting the stronghold existed in early August, or, if it did, whether the Davises knew anything of it. However, other reports of trail conditions, like Cain's, if they existed, may have provided the impulse for the Davises to reevaluate their situation and state of readiness for the remainder of their journey. Such a reevaluation may have caused them to change course and head to Salt Lake City to resupply, rest, and perhaps gather information — though there is nothing in Sarah's diary suggesting it. Furthermore, they and their company seemed alone in their southern decision—unlikely if there was general knowledge of a significant problem on the trail ahead. Therefore, while it is possible trail conditions played a part in their decision to turn south, it seems very unlikely.

Economics, then, becomes the most likely cause for the abrupt shift in direction. The Davises presumably left Michigan to seek the increased opportunity and riches the West had to offer. Zeno, a gunsmith, required concentrations of people and their hardware to prosper. The goldfields of California offered such concentrations, as did a rapidly growing Salt Lake City—the only city between St. Joseph and California. In 1850 over 11,000 residents lived in Salt Lake City,[6] the University of Utah was established, the Deseret News started publishing on a weekly basis, and the Utah Territory was created with its seat in Salt Lake City. Salt Lake City was a growing enterprise—just the sort of place a young blacksmith and his family could make a stand. Perhaps the Davises thought it would be worth taking a look at the city to see what opportunity it could promise.

Whichever the reason, their decision carried considerable risk, and they would not have made it lightly. Travelers to California had a narrow window of time to make the trip. If they left too early, the grass was too thin to provide adequate feed; if they left too late, or spent too much time on the trail, they risked snow and winter by the time they reached the Sierra Nevada (as it turns out, they arrived at the Sierra Nevada in a snow storm).[7] They must have known that turning south where and when they did would add days, if not weeks, to their journey. Assuming they understood the implications of this, their objective, whatever it was, must have seemed worth the risk.

Snow and cold were not strangers on their trip. Since leaving St. Joseph, they slowly ascended the gradual slope of the Great Plains, adding just over ninety feet of elevation a day. By the time they reached Fort Laramie, they had gained 3,300 feet. When they reached central Wyoming they were consistently at altitudes over 6,000 feet and crossing passes and ridges greater than 8,000 feet. Adding more muscle to the chill, they were gaining in latitude; on 11 July, near today's Glenrock, Wyoming, they reached their journey's maximum latitude of 42.9°N. Moreover, the middle of the nineteenth century presented some of the lowest temperatures of that era's "Little Ice Age."[8] Latitude, elevation, and an ice age conspired to create extremely chilly conditions for summer travelers. Emigrants reported cold nights and mornings, breaking ice in water casks, freezing rain, snow-covered peaks, and snow banks along the trail. Sarah frequently mentioned "snowy," or "snow," mountains and "vary" cold nights and mornings.

The Rocky Mountains were surely the most amazing and colorful part of their entire trip. They passed Independence Rock, Devil's Gate, Sweetwater Rocks, two deserts, and multiple rivers. They skirted the Laramie and Wind River Ranges, crossed the Continental Divide, traversed several high ridges, ate snow in July, saw enormous fields of wildflowers, encountered several bands of Native Americans, and witnessed a man whipped almost to death.

*　　　*　　　*

Sunday, 30 June 1850.

> **june 30　we came to larimy fork and then we crost it   it is the swiftest riveer I ever saw but not vary wide   when we crost it we went a half mile and camped**

Their camping location, after traveling twenty-two miles, was one-half mile northwest of their ford across the Laramie River and along the Platte.

Monday, 1 July. Sarah combined the 1 July and 2 July entries into a single, 1 July, diary entry. The relevant day is in bold text.

> **july 1   we camped near fourte lairimy and then we washed we staid till july 2 and wased** and then we went on to fourte lairimy and past it six miles   we then staid one day and wased and baked again and

They remained in their camp near the fort.

Tuesday, 2 July 1850.

> july 1   we camped near fourte lairimy and then we washed we staid till july 2 and wased **and then we went on to fourte lairimy and past it six miles   we then staid one day and wased and baked again and**

Their location was six miles past their previous day's location.

Wednesday, 3 July 1850.

> *july 3 we laid on the plat*

Thursday, 4 July 1850 (Sarah and Zeno's wedding anniversary).

> *july 4 we camped near to one of the best springs I ever saw* [Warm Springs] *but litle gras for our Catle we are now in the rockey mountains and it is rockey mountains for certain t[h]eir is some of the largest rocks I ever saw t[h]eir are some large pine trees here and some cedar tree and plenty of lime stone we started on the next day and left mr janson behind hear as one of his men was sick*

Eight miles found them at Warm Springs. From here, they began an eighty-mile stretch of the trail that does not follow the banks of the Platte.[9] This route, sometimes called the "Black Hills Route," took a more direct line northwest toward Deer Creek and bypassed two large arcs of the Platte (See maps 12 and 13).[10] They came to the Platte again on 11 July.

Friday, 5 July 1850.

> *july 5 friday we went on and past too handsome creeks one was biter creek* [current-day Cottonwood Creek] *it had some butifull fish in it we then past dead timber creek* [current-day Little Cottonwood Creek] *and nooned near the bluffs we now had to pass seven miles with out timber or water we then got to timber but no water but in alittle while we had plenty of water their came a tremendous thunder souer and come rushing down the hills in greate fountains like the waves from the lake they came in too feete high* [Sarah is referring to the waves of Lake Michigan; Sarah's home in Michigan was just east of Lake Michigan.]

This day took them west along Bitter (Cottonwood) Creek, then northwest up a large canyon from the intersection of today's

Interstate 25 and Cottonwood Creek. Their camping location, after traveling nearly twenty-four miles, was along a small creek two miles to the west of current-day Table Mountain.

Saturday, 6 July 1850.

july saturday 6 we started on and traveled eight miles and then nooned   we past holer spring to day and horse creek [current-day Horseshoe Creek] *we had no grass or our catle to day noon and hardly any to night   we camped on a dry creek* [current-day North Elkhorn Creek].

After traveling fourteen miles, they spent the night along the banks of today's North Elkhorn Creek.

Sunday, 7 July 1850.

july 7 sunday we started on and traveled eight miles   we stoped to noon on lebonte [a la Bonté[11]] *river whare we had no grass for our catle we then went on and camped on a branch of the lebonte river five miles farther on* [today's Wagonhound Creek] *whare their was toads with thornes and tails   their was a man died their that night and was baried next morning I had almost forgoten that they kiled too buffalow and what a supper we had plenty*

After thirteen miles, they spent this night at current-day Wagonhound Creek.

Monday, 8 July 1850.

july 8 monday we traveled a bout eight miles and stoped to noon we then went on to a lee perle river and camped for the night   it was vary colde water and clear   we lost one of our cous

Their location, after traveling another thirteen miles, was at the bank of the La Prele River.

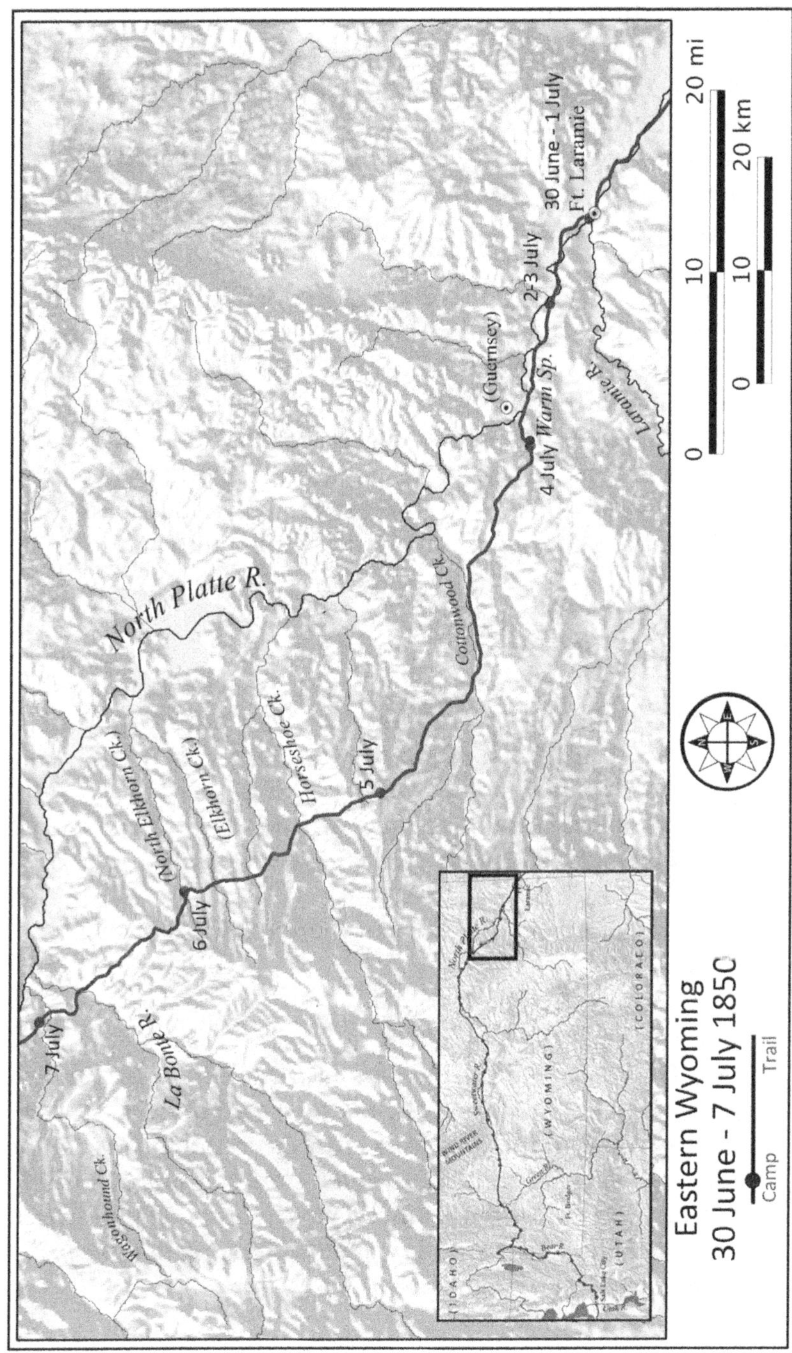

Map 12. Eastern Wyoming.

Tuesday, 9 July 1850.

> *july 9 tuesday   we started on and traveled to box elder creek and stoped to noon   whilst we ware their their hapened to come a long a bufalo a bounding like a deer only a great deal more[12]   we traveled on to fous bois creek and stoped for the night*

There are two Box Elder Creeks on current maps. The first, the Little Box Elder Creek, was where Sarah and Zeno nooned and is just over five miles from the La Prele River.[13] The second Box Elder Creek intersects the trail three miles farther west still. William Clayton, an emigrant, diarist, and route gazetteer described this second creek as the Fourche Boise River.[14] This river also appears on the 1846 Preuss map as the Fourche Boisée (Figure 8).[15] The Davises camped on the ninth and tenth at this river.

Wednesday, 10 July 1850.

> *july 10 we stoped at fous bois river a butifull stream the water was clear as cristal and it had plenty of fish in it we spent one day their a washing and baking   those that could be spared went a hunting and to of them killed a buffalo and too others killed a black tailed deer we had plesent time of it their*

They remained on the banks of the Fourche Boisée.

Thursday, 11 July 1850.

> *july 11 friday we started on and traveled fourteen miles   we then cameped on deer creek one of butifull creeks I ever saw plenty of fish in it and it is as clear as cristal and as cold as ice their is a spring here that as much colder as you can think we have a butifull camping place plenty of wood and water and a good shade   I saw too large buffalo to day and the men after them was same*

After traveling nine miles, the Davises camped at the intersection of the trail and Deer Creek in today's Glenrock, Wyoming. Clayton describes this location as a "lovely place to camp."[16] There is a small note at the top of the diary's page, "deer creak 1314," which explains the lack of entries and where the Davises were on the thirteenth and fourteenth. Sarah and her party spent three nights at Deer Creek.

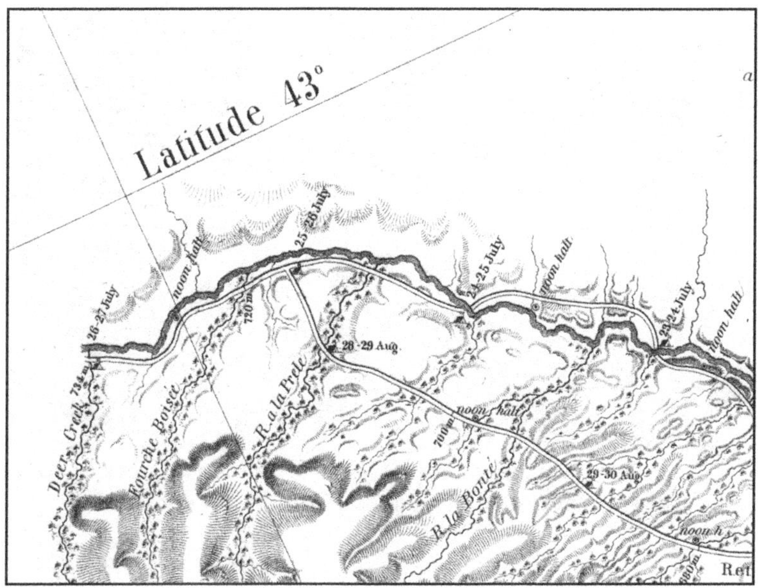

Figure 8. A segment of the 1846 Preuss map depicting the Fourche Boisée, or current-day Box Elder Creek. (Library of Congress.)

Friday, 12 July 1850.

july 12 we still lay here a herding our catle and Zeno went out this morning before breakefast and a antelope and returned before noon the rest the men killed nothing of any consequence o yes mr mclelen killed a buffalo and to grouse we still lay here at deer creek we lay here three days recruiting ["renewal or repair of something worn out"[17]] *our catle they got so that they ware perfectly crazy*

Saturday and Sunday, 13 and 14 July 1850.

They remained at Deer Creek.

Figure 9. Possible Deer Creek camping area in Glenrock, Wyoming (now a Glenrock city park). (Camera location: 42.8648°N 105.8663°W facing east.)

Monday, 15 July 1850.

> *july 15 we started on and traveled on to the plat whare their was a grove of timber* [Clayton puts this grove nine and one-quarter miles from Deer Creek.[18]] *it was coten wood and their noned mr mclelan and Edwin went out to git some of his buffalo meat in the morning and did not return till we nooned on the plat and when they returned they had killed a nother and braught in some meat with them and then we traveled tulve miles*

Their location, after twenty-one miles traveling, was in current-day Evansville, Wyoming.

Tuesday, 16 July 1850.

> *july 16 we camped on the plat river and then we started and to a litle creek within one mile of the forde and nooned there we went on and crost ferry and camped just a crost river we then left river*

After traveling seven miles, they arrived at the river crossing in current-day Casper, Wyoming. They crossed the Platte to camp on its northern side.

Wednesday, 17 July 1850.

> *july 17 we are now crosing a desert we come to a mineral lake and spring then we to some low land hily [highly] charged with alcholie we then come to a spring and water our catle and git some super and then traveled all night our catle ware nearly worne out not having any grass since we left the plat nearly fifty miles*

They were moving through the "desert" between Casper, Wyoming, and Independence Rock. The stream Sarah mentions is probably Willow Spring, the first reliable water source found after leaving the Casper area.

Thursday, 18 July 1850.

> *july 18 we camped on cottonwood creek and staid all day to feed our catle they not having any thing to eat for the last seventy miles of any consequence we staid all day their*

After traveling forty-six miles, they arrived at current-day Dry Creek. One of this stream's tributaries, several miles to the north, is Cottonwood Creek.

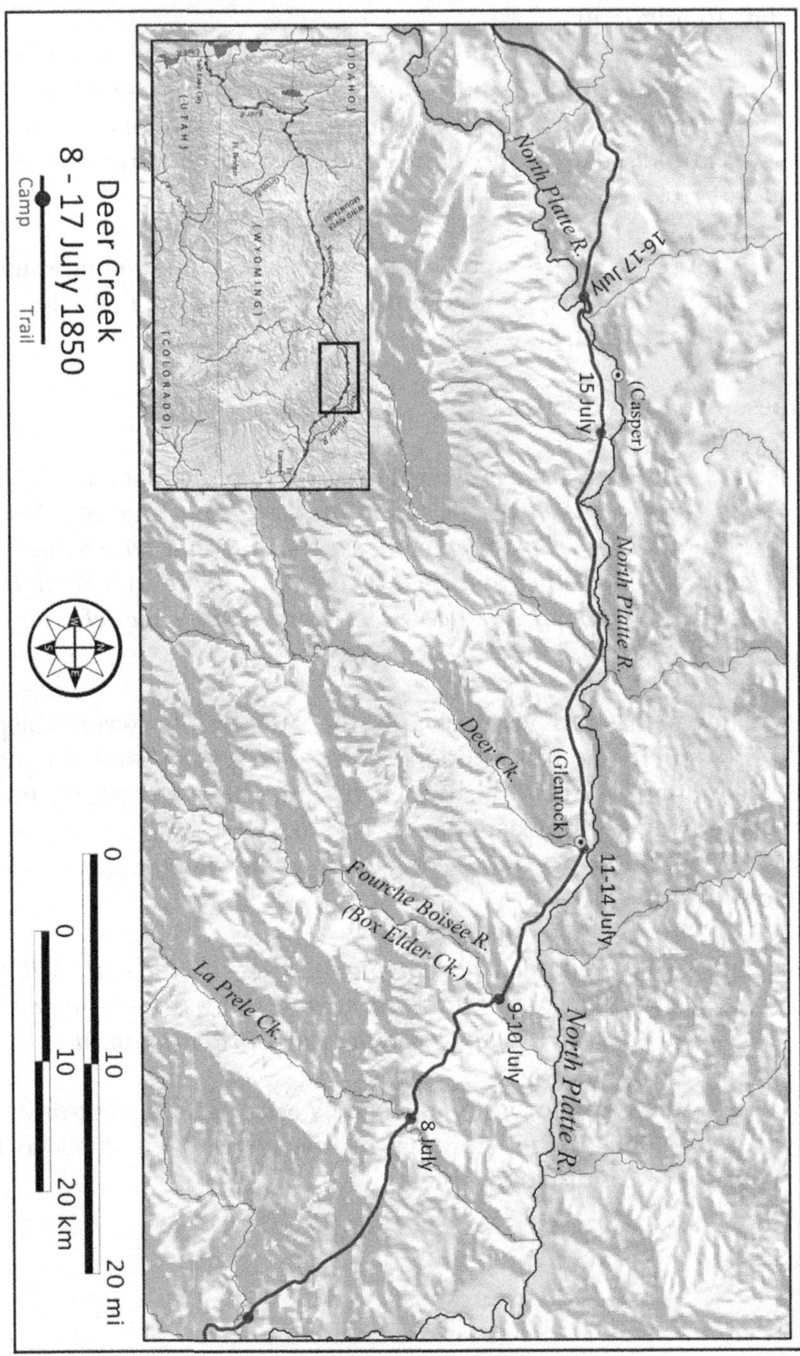

Map 13. Deer Creek.

Figure 10. Willow Springs. (Camera location: 42.6743°N 106.7930°W facing north.)

Friday, 19 July 1850.

> *july 19   we started on and traveled to independence rock and their stoped to noon   their is the most names onit I ever saw in my life   the rock is completly covered with names as far as I can see and a greeat many serched out to put theirs their   mr Estus braught me some curents from top of it   there is plenty of them here   we have now arived at the sweete river water*

Their location was just over fifteen miles past their Cottonwood Creek camp. They nooned at Independence Rock, then traveled along the Sweetwater, past the "Devil's Gate," then camped along a tributary stream with good water.[19]

Sarah is referring to currants when she mentions curents. A currant, which ripens in July, is a berry common to this area.[20]

Saturday, 20 July 1850.

> *july 20 we camped on the sweete water river and to men staid with us   with us I say they staid with our company   we have plenty of good water here*

After traveling only nine miles, they camped on Sage Creek (current-day Willow Creek), a source of water.[21] They remained here the night of the twenty-first as well.

Figure 11. Independence Rock, Wyoming. (Camera location: 42.4937°N 107.1369°W facing east.)

Sunday, 21 July 1850.

> *july 21 sunday we staid on the suete water and the men drove our catle to grass in the mountains five miles from here and a mr steelle[22] who was with them killed a bull Elk but he braught none of it in   we found plenty of goosbury here of the best kind I ever saw in my life I think the sueete water is a butifull stream it is clear and rapid   their is no large fish in it as we have found yet I expect their is plenty but the*[y] [the men] *being busy they had no time* [to fish.]

Monday, 22 July 1850.

> *july 22 monday morning we started on and traveled six miles and stoped to noon having traveled through heavy sand all the way we have now past biter coten wood a dismal lookin place it is we had vary sandy rodes all the afternoon*

Ten miles brought them to a camping spot south of the Sweetwater and west of Bitter Cottonwood Creek.

Tuesday, 23 July 1850.

> *july 23 we camped on the sueete water and vary good rodes all day we crost the river four times and traveled thirteen miles we past through mountains whare the rock was three hundred feete high on both sides of us and the river past betwene them I saw three buffalo to day*

After traveling fourteen miles, the Davises camped in the current-day Sweetwater Rocks area. Sarah's description of this day's journey closely matches that of Clayton's. Both Sarah and Clayton agree that there are four crossings, they pass through some very high mountains, and the roads are good on the north side of the river.[23]

Wednesday, 24 July 1850.

> *july 24 we camped on the sueete water and drove our catle three miles to grass we have a butifull campin place here and vary plesent eavning and morning the catle are now coming and must qit riting we have to pass through sixteen miles of desert to day we have now got through the desert and crost the seete water and now we camp here their is not much grass here for our catle*

From their camping spot on the twenty-third, they traveled a seventeen-mile diagonal to bypass a bend in the river.[24]

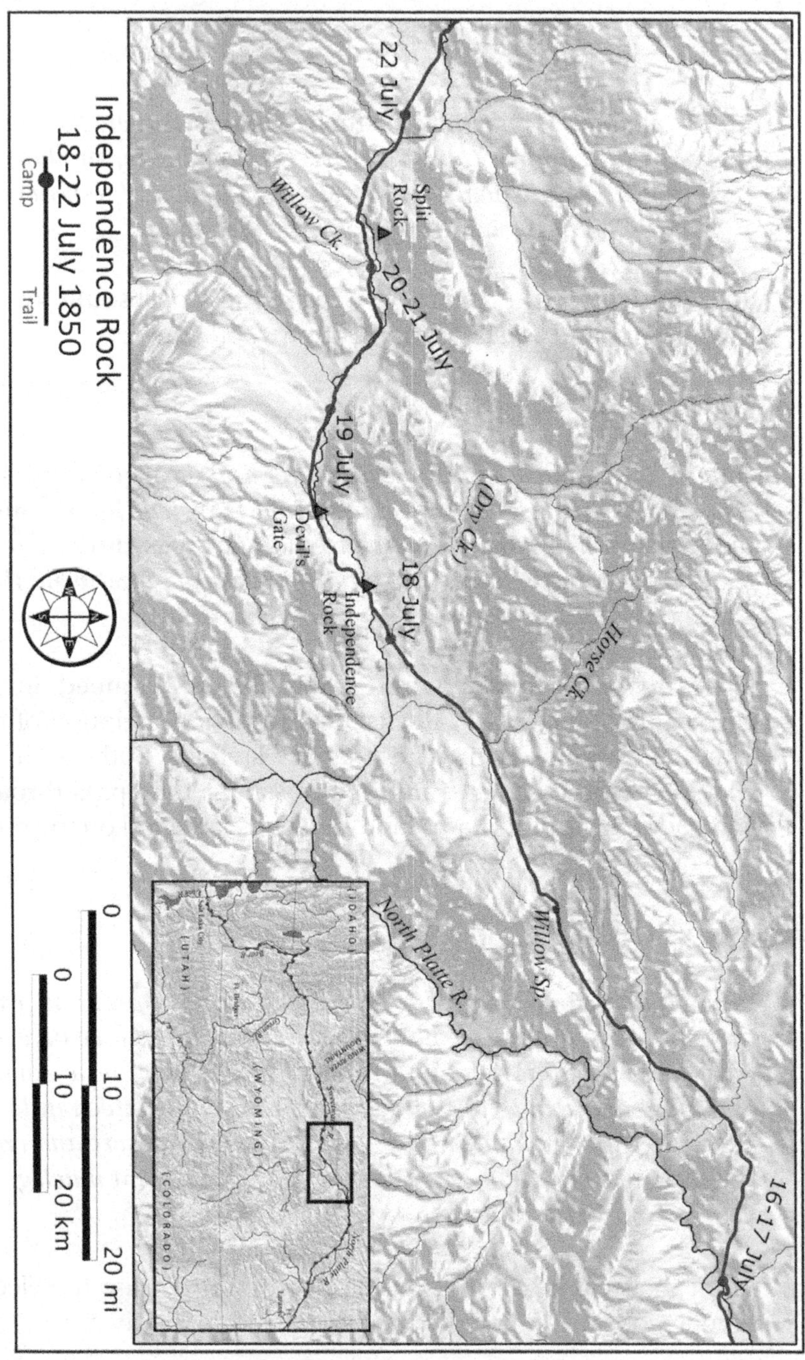

Map 14. Independence Rock.

Figure 12. Looking west through the "twin mounds."[25]
(Camera location: 42.3472°N 108.8303°W facing west.)

Thursday, 25 July 1850.

> *july 25 we traveled twenty miles to day   we have crost too small creeks* [Silver Creek and Deep Creek] *and past the twin mounts*[26] *and too alcholie lakes* [Lewiston Lakes] *and sevrel rockey ridges   we can see the rockey mountains* [the Wind River Range][27] *which is coverd with snow and they look whit a little   I think we have now crost strubry creek and camped for the night*

Their location, after traveling twenty miles, was along the southern bank of Strawberry Creek.[28]

Friday, 26 July 1850.

> *july 26 we camped on seete water for the last time just opposite of the snow mountain* [Sarah is referring to the Wind River Mountains.] *and it was vary colde   we past twin mountains*

they are [not] *vary high* [twin mounds (Figure 12)[29]] *we have had plenty of snow to eat here on the seete water we nooned on the sueete water to day* [The trail intersects the Sweetwater about halfway through this day's journey.] *we have traveled nine teen miles to day and now we are at the south pass*

This is the last time the Davises will see the Sweetwater River. Here, just east of the South Pass, the Sweetwater River, flowing in from the north, turns to the east. This turn, or elbow, provided a likely spot to camp eighteen miles from their previous camping spot.

For the last couple of days, Sarah has commented on the weather turning colder. Their elevation (almost 7,500 feet) and latitude (42.5°N) are both quite high. John Steele (another Emigrant and author), who crossed over the South Pass two weeks earlier on 13 July, also reported snow banks along the trail.[30]

Figure 13. The remarkably un-remarkable South Pass. (Camera location: 42.3491°N 108.8868°W facing west.)

Saturday, 27 July 1850.

july 27   we are now in the south pass past the pacific springs and stoped to noon   we now stop to camp on the dry sandy distance from pacific five miles   it rains considerable and it is vary colde almost cold and enuf to freeze [freeze, "realize" is in someone else's hand, possibly Power's]   *I think a* [the day's narrative ends]

After sixteen miles of travel on a cold, rainy day, the Davises set up camp along the banks of Dry Sandy Creek.

[second entry for 27 July] *july 27   we traveled nine teen miles then we stoped on the sueete water for the last time   we stoped near a train of twenty wagons traders a goin to salt lake nothing more transpired of any consequence*

The author is unsure where this entry fits in the geographical narrative. In a geographic sense, it seems to repeat the 26 July entry. Accordingly, this day's information was not added to the distances, and no new camping location is reckoned. However, this entry does point to an awareness of the path to Salt Lake City.

Sunday, 28 July 1850.

july 28   we went on to little sandy distance of tuelve miles and then stoped for the day and to grase our catle   we had to drove them five miles to grase and whilst the men ware gone with the catle this large train come in one mile of us and camped their a rose a quarrel with them and ofal qureling I never heard the like   they were whipping a man for whipping his wife   he had whipped her every day since he joined the company and now they thaught it was time for them to whip him and they caught him and striped him and took the ox gad to him and whipped him tremenduous she scremed and hollered for him till she might have hare him for three miles   the little sandy is vary mudy and bout forty feet wide with suift current

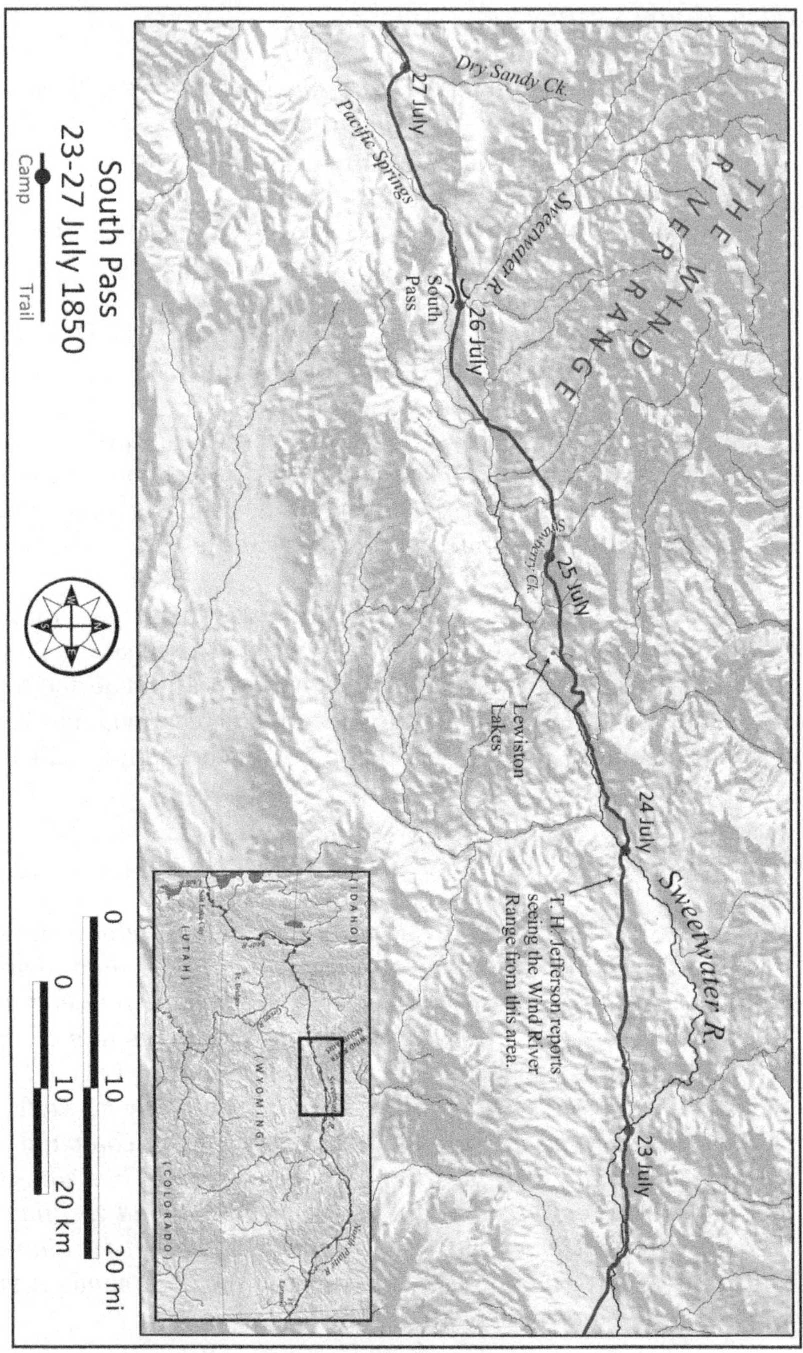

Map 15. Through the South Pass.

After traveling ten miles, the Davises camped on the banks of the Little Sandy River. On this day they passed the Parting of the Ways.

At this juncture, it is important to establish which direction the Davises took, as here they were confronted with a choice of two trails. The first, the Oregon-California Trail, headed southwest to Fort Bridger, thence northwest to the Bear River valley (along what is sometimes called the "Fort Hall Road"[31]) and Thomas' Fork (or, if Salt Lake City was the object, travelers continued past Fort Bridger along the Hastings Cutoff over the Wasatch Mountains into Salt Lake City). The second, the Sublette Cutoff, bypassed Fort Bridger by striking a more westerly course across the Green River drainage to the Bear River valley where the cutoff ends and rejoins the Oregon-California Trail (along the Fort Hall Road), then north to Thomas' Fork.

A traveler heading for California or Oregon could take either trail. The main Oregon-California Trail taken southwest to Fort Bridger, then northwest to Thomas' Fork was longer but avoided a forty-one mile desert.[32] The Sublette Cutoff was shorter, but travelers were confronted with the desert. The Sublette Cutoff was more popular; David Lavender, a noted historian, contends that in 1849 about half of the emigrants traveled the Sublette, and John Caughey, another noted historian, estimates that nine of eleven emigrants took the Sublette in 1850.[33]

Sarah's description of her journey matches the Sublette Cutoff. Sarah described leaving the Big Sandy River and then spending a night and day traveling across a desert to reach the Green River (29-30 July). This description matches the physical terrain (as well as several guidebooks) found between the Big Sandy and the Green Rivers along the Sublette Cutoff.

Past the Green, Sarah's diary entries continue to maintain their close match to the Sublette Cutoff terrain. Leaving the Green River, Sarah described a trip of thirteen miles to a branch of the Green; the physical terrain produces the Fontenelle at twelve miles. The next day's (2 August) thirteen-mile journey had them traveling through the "Rocky Gap" to spend the night in the Pomeroy Basin; though Sarah doesn't record a distance, she does describe traveling between two "snow mountains" to establish a camp on this same day. From the Pomeroy Basin, it is another ten miles to Ham's Fork; on 3 August, Sarah describes the beauty of Ham's Fork valley after ten miles travel. Her narrative continues to match the terrain and their position in it along the Sublette Cutoff to the Bear River (the Sublette's end) and north to Thomas' Fork.

On the other hand, if we assume they did not take the Sublette Cutoff and traveled to Fort Bridger, then we are immediately presented with the problem of the "desert" that Sarah describes preparing for and crossing. A desert requiring two days and a night to cross does not exist along the route to Fort Bridger. Travelers heading to Fort Bridger followed the Dry Sandy, crossed over the Little Sandy, followed its bank to and crossed the Big Sandy, then followed the Big Sandy's bank, more or less, all the way to the Green River. Guidebooks recommended pioneers travel seventeen miles to good water and grass after crossing the Big Sandy, so an all-night and all-day sojourn was not required to reach water. Another ten miles farther produced the Green River itself.[34] Furthermore, if, along this Fort Bridger route, we assume they left their camp on the Green River on 1 August (when Sarah states they left the Green), then the next river they would encounter that same day would have been Ham's Fork; yet, this river doesn't appear in Sarah's diary until 3 August. The next river after Ham's Fork would have been Black's Fork, which Sarah doesn't mention at all. Continuing would bring them to Fort Bridger, which Sarah also fails to mention. Since Sarah mentioned the preceding two forts as well as all the major rivers they encountered, it is likely she would have mentioned Fort Bridger situated on Black's Fork — she did not.

Comparing her diary entries and the physical terrain, it is clear the Davises took the Sublette Cutoff. In both time and space, Sarah's descriptions of the desert to the Green River, the Fontenelle, Ham's Fork, the Bear River, and arriving at Thomas' Fork all match well with the physical terrain as well as others' descriptions of the Sublette Cutoff. Moreover, her same descriptions match poorly with terrain along the Oregon-California Trail to Fort Bridger.[35]

Monday, 29 July 1850.

> *july 29 we started on and traveled a bout tuelve mles   we then crost big sandy   it too hundred feet wide with suift current and vary mudy   we then parted with some our company their mr crouses and one mr mires and mr hunter and mr jonson and harter and three mr Estuss and mr wilams and mr heiple and burg   some of the best men I ever got a acqanted with   I think they went to california and we go to oregon   we parted about noon[36] we then on to big sandy and then camped for the night in a butifull place*

Their location is along the Sublette Trail on the western bank of the Big Sandy River.

Tuesday, 30 July 1850.

> *july 30   we encamped on the big sandy and some of our men washed and some of them baked   we baked and fixed for the desert of thirty five miles   we start to night for the desert   one of our men lost one of his oxen with this alcolie and some of elicks is sick   mr stell lost one of his cous yesterday   we have now eat diner and are all most ready to start   this is a butiful place to camp* [Joseph Ware, a period guidebook author, cautions that cattle can get sick in this area due to alkali water.[37]]

They remained at their Big Sandy camp through the night of the twenty-ninth and day of the thirtieth, preparing for the desert by filling every vessel with water and letting the cattle rest. They started to cross the desert on the evening of the thirtieth.

Wednesday, 31 July 1850.

> *july 31 we traveled all night and come to green river a distance of thirty five miles   we then crost the river and camped for the night   we drove our catle five miles to grass   there is plenty of fish in this river   there is a fery here* [Mountain men established ferry crossings along the Green years before 1850.[38]] *this river is clear and suift current   the river is thirty rods wide   I saw*

six snake Indians   here they cary a white feather with them   a sign of pease   they look fright full

After traveling forty-one miles through the moonlit night of the thirtieth and the day of the thirty-first, they crossed the Green River and camped.[39]

Figure 14. Possible Green River crossing area at the base of current-day Steed Canyon. (Camera location: 42.2006°N 110.1543°W facing south.)

Thursday, 1 August 1850.

august 1   we left green river and crost over the mountain [today's Holden Hill] *a distance of thireen miles   we then come on to a branch of greene river* [Fontenelle Creek] *a butifull stream it is   we camped on it and we past some Indians   snake Indians*

After traveling twelve miles, they camped on the south side of Fontenelle Creek.

Friday, 2 August 1850.

*august 2   we nooned in sight of an Indian town   we then come
on eight miles and in betwene too snow mountains   within an
Indian camp their was to m[o]re camps in sight*

Sixteen miles past their 1 August camp and after passing
through the Rocky Gap, the Davises camped along Willow
Creek in current-day Pomeroy Basin, situated between the
Commissary and Oyster Ridges.

Saturday, 3 August 1850.

*august 3   we then started on and traveled ten miles to good
grass and it was good grass to for it ne high to a man   we then
come to hams fork of greene river   a beautifull stream   it runs
vary suift and is clear as cristal   it is a bout three rods wide
and has plent of trout in it   here is and Indian town   they
swarmed around us   it is the snake tribe of Indians who in
habit these snoue mountains   they lok fright full*

After ten miles, the Davises descended into the strikingly
beautiful Ham's Fork valley.

Sunday, 4 August 1850.

*august 4   we lay buy all day here to rest our catle and wash
and bake   our men took off on of their wgons covrs und soucd
them together and used it for a sane* [seine — a fishing net[40]]
*they had lots of fun hre   they caught about too thousan fish
with big little and all to gether   there is gossbarys here and
sratibey* [strawberry] *here and some butifull roses and pine in a
bundance   we had plenty of wilows for wood*

Monday, 5 August 1850.

*august 5 we then started on our catle bein all fresh   we then
commence to clime the mountains   I saw whre we had to go
before starting and had the sick head ache   vary bad   I saw*

nothing at all the four noon   In the after noon a more butifull sight I never saw   the hole mountain was covered with fours of every description you could think of   we past through a fur grove of timber   it was butifull and groves of qaken aspen [Three miles after crossing Ham's Fork, the trail follows a ridgeline paralleling current-day "Quakenasp Canyon."]

After traveling sixteen miles, the Davises camped along Rock Creek between the Dempsey and Oyster Ridges. At this point, the Sublette Cutoff splits into three forks: a northern, middle, and southern.[41] Each fork heads west and intersects the Bear River four miles distant from each other. Based strictly on correlation with distances, the author has chosen the middle fork as the one the party followed; "we then past over mountains for six miles…" is coincident with the measured mileage from Rock Creek to the Bear along this middle fork.

Sarah seems to have shifted her diary entries here. She is now recording a night's camping location on the next day's diary entry. For instance, for this day, the fifth, she tells us about the camping location in her 6 August entry: "we camped on the mountain side a butifull stream running benith it we then passed…"

Tuesday, 6 August 1850.

august 6   we camped [on the fifth] *on the mountain side a butifull stream runing beneath it   the current suift and clear it was mudy buy name we then past over mountains for six miles and then we came in bare river bottom and their we had a runaway   our catle run and the leader fell doun and that stoped them   nothing got broke   we then went on to the river and nooned   the Indians sarmed a round*

After they left Rock Creek, the Davises crossed Rock Creek Ridge and then followed current-day Sublette Creek and Trail Creek to the Bear River. Arrival at the Bear River marked the end of the Sublette Cutoff as they now joined the Fort Hall Road heading north to Thomas' Fork. Following the Fort Hall Road north for fifteen miles brought them to Thomas' Fork, where

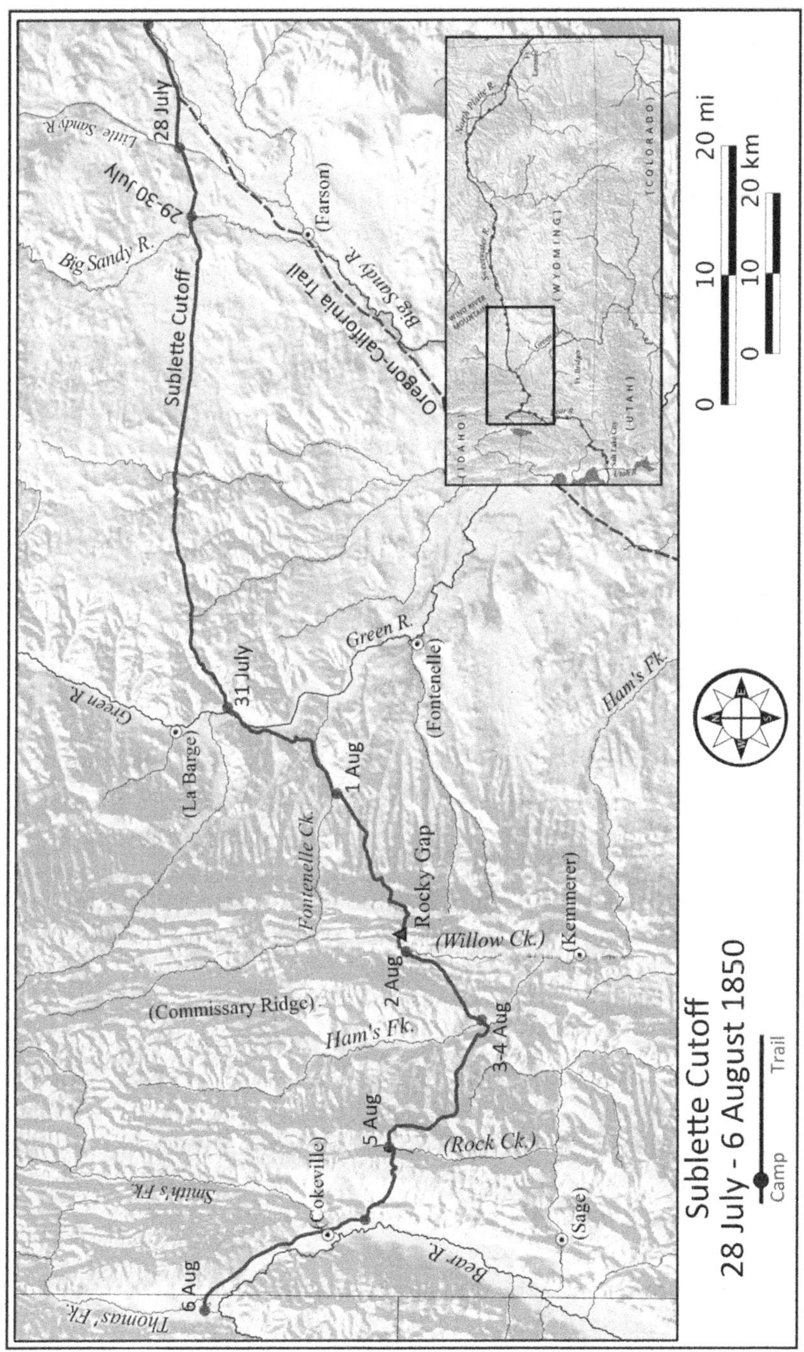

Map 16. Sublette Cutoff.

they camped for the evening (described in Sarah's 7 August diary entry). They traveled twenty-one miles this day.

Wednesday, 7 August 1850.

august 7 we camped [on the night of the sixth] *on Thomas fork of the bare river   we then parted with the rest of our company and turned rounde to go too salt lake   evry body we past they aked are you turned back   my what is the mater   why dont you go on   we then come on ten miles and stoped to noon on bare river   their was one Indian come to us for his diner   we then went on for five or six miles and stoped to camp   we camped all a lone   it seamed vary lonely*

Having made the decision to travel to Salt Lake, they turned around and retraced their steps along the Fort Hall Road for fifteen miles before spending the evening near the same spot where they met the Fort Hall Road on the sixth.

Thursday, 8 August 1850.

august 8   we then went on the fourte briger road for ten miles and stoped to camp   we past to of the best Springs I ever saw in my life

Ten miles south of their 7 August campsite and along the Fort Hall Road put them abreast of current-day Antelope Creek.

Friday, 9 August 1850.

august 9   we started on to salt lake   we went back five miles on the road and have not come to the road yet   we went on a bout seven miles farther whare we stoped to camp and yet we are not in sight of the road   the boys killed four ducks which made us a handsome mess for breckfast

Seven miles past their 8 August camp spot put them on the Fort Hall Road at the banks of Twin Creek. They seem to be trying to find a road. What road are they looking for? It is doubtful they lost the Fort Hall Road. As early as 1843, the explorer John C. Frémont described the Fort Hall Road as an "excellent road."[42] By 1850, this road was a well-established wagon road. It is only dimly possible that they lost such a well-used trail during daylight and presumably in clear weather. Is there another road or trail, perhaps heading south, up the Bear River that would take them to the Hastings Cutoff?

From a time and distance standpoint, this proposition makes some sense. If we establish the Davises at Twin Creek on the ninth and take Sarah's word for her mileage calculations, then we can trace the ten miles they traveled on the tenth aside the western slope of today's Crawford Mountains and eastern bank of the Bear River until they were near current-day Larson Spring. They camped there for two days (11 and 12 August) presumably attempting to locate a road. On the thirteenth Sarah tells us they traveled about fifteen miles, placing them just past the southern tip of the Crawford Mountains and at a likely fording spot of the Bear River.

Though Sarah gives no mileage for the fourteenth, she gives both an identifiable camping location (Hastings Cutoff and Echo Creek intersection) and distance traveled on the fifteenth, twenty miles. From this information, we can establish their camping location on the fourteenth (twenty miles back from the fifteenth's camp) in the Bear River valley about three miles north of Yellow Creek's mouth and sixteen miles south of their 13 August camping spot. On the next day, the fifteenth, they covered those twenty miles by traveling south along the Bear, veering right to follow the Yellow Creek, "finding the [Hastings Cutoff] road," then following Hastings Cutoff west to their Echo Creek camp. Sarah's recorded distance (including the implied sixteen miles on the fourteenth) to Echo Creek following this Bear River path is fifty-nine miles, which is reasonably close to the path's measured mileage.

On the other hand, had they followed the Fort Hall Road to Fort Bridger, linking up with the Hastings Cutoff there, then traveled west to Echo Creek, they would have traveled a distance of about one hundred miles. Sarah's recorded mileages are short by about forty miles equating to two or three days travel.

Based on her descriptions of the countryside, the Bear River valley route makes sense as well. Throughout the journey from the ninth to the fourteenth, Sarah was impressed with the quality of the grass she encountered, described as "nee high" and the "handsomest grass I ever saw in my life." Sarah also described an abundance of antelope, ducks, and geese. These attributes fit well with a description of a large river valley of the West. Moreover, it seems she was specifically describing the Bear River valley of the mid 1800s. Frémont likewise described this valley as rich with "common blue flax growing abundantly…," and "…luxuriant pasturage," as well as seeing "…antelope and elk…during the day…; and…ducks and geese in the river."[43] Lastly, Sarah describes traveling "*up* [emphasis added] the river." The Bear River in this area flows north, so traveling south along its banks is, in fact, traveling up the river.

Alternatively, the physical attributes of the Fort Hall Road southeast of Bridger Creek (where this road leaves the Bear River valley) are considerably different than Sarah's descriptions. This route presented travelers with tough, mountainous terrain. Ware describes this road as "crooked and sometimes steep, passing between high mountains. Water is scarce during this distance."[44] Granted, they would reach larger rivers along this route (the Muddy Fork and Black's Fork) that support Sarah's described conditions, but to get to these rivers meant crossing the Bear River Divide, which immediately presented a climb of almost 1,500 feet. Frémont, traveling the opposite direction, described the descent of this hill as "…rather precipitous."[45] Several other ridgelines would follow before flatter terrain fit the ingredients of Sarah's descriptions. Sarah, who faithfully mentioned virtually any hill (perhaps because she suffered at higher altitudes), mentions nothing of these rugged ridges.

Between the ninth and the fifteenth, Sarah's diary entries are virtually devoid of human activity extraneous to her party; she only mentions one other human and a single human enterprise, a campsite. This makes sense, as this route up the Bear River was not and would not become one of the trails followed by pioneers heading west. They are taking this route only because they felt compelled to travel to Salt Lake City after their arrival at the Thomas' Fork. Sarah's repeated admissions of being "vary lonely" are entirely consistent with a Bear River path.

On the other hand, if they had followed the Fort Hall Road to Fort Bridger, it is likely they would have seen more signs of human activity considering the tens of thousands of people traveling to California during the gold rush years.[46] If even a fraction of this number moved north along the Fort Hall Road in 1850, then Sarah's party would have encountered more than one other traveler and one camping spot. Furthermore, Sarah, who was faithful in pointing out trading posts, native camps, and both previous forts surely would have mentioned Fort Bridger, which, as described by another emigrant, Lucena Parsons in September 1850, was "composed of 4 log houses and a small enclosure for horses…[with] many Indian huts in sight";[47] Sarah mentioned nothing of the fort.

While there is much to suggest they did travel south up the Bear River valley, such a cross-country trip carried some risk. They probably had little idea of the conditions, roads, trails, or native activities. Of course, this area wasn't completely unexplored. The local natives surely had a keen understanding of this area, and there may have been some local, non-Native American, knowledge as well. Still, the only previous well known account of a white man traveling south up the Bear River in this area was Jedediah Smith in 1827. Smith entered the valley from the west (from the southern tip of Bear Lake), then traveled south, past what became the Hastings Cutoff, and then turned toward the Weber River probably at Chalk Creek.[48]

The safe bet was for the Davises to have taken the Fort Hall road up and over the mountains, through Fort Bridger, then turn west along the Hastings Cutoff to Salt Lake. Such a route would be easier to accept, however, if there was evidence to show that this was the course Sarah and her party took. The evidence, distances and time, physical description, and human activity all point to a trip up the Bear River valley. Therefore, barring any other note to the contrary, it is more probable the Davises left Thomas' Fork, headed south up the Bear River valley until reaching the Hastings Cutoff where they turned west to Echo Creek.

Saturday, 10 August 1850.

> *august 10 we started on and traveled some eight miles   we then stoped to noon and zeno and Alick went to look for the road I am vary lonely and wish we could find the road we lay buy the rest of the day ad not founde the road yet*

After eight miles, the Davises established a camp between current-day Crawford Mountains and the Bear River in the vicinity of today's Larson Spring.

Sunday, 11 August 1850.

> *august 11 we lay buy all day and nothing transpired of any consequence   I think it a long time*

Monday, 12 August 1850.

> *august 21 [12] we still lay her and no hopes of giting a way about four o clock Elick and Edwin come back and they had found the road & how I rejoiced to think they had found the road they brought home aleven ducks with them and we had fine mess of them   mr mclelen and mr burten they went a hunting to day and they killed eleven more ducks   we had a plenty of them*

Tuesday, 13 August 1850.

> *august 13 we started on up the river to find the road and past through plenty of grass nee high we stoped to noon in a butiful place and Zeno killed a goose   it was younge and beter meat I never eat in my life we then went on and I think we traveled fifteen miles that day   we ware raerly out of sight of antelope all day*

In this pivotal entry, Sarah describes traveling *up* stream, "nee high" grass, geese, and antelope. If they were traveling to Fort Bridger, this day's diary entry would likely mention the travails of crossing the Bear River Divide and subsequent ridgelines; it does not. This entry's description does, however, mirror conditions likely found in the Bear River valley of 1850. Fifteen miles travel put the Davises camp past the southern tip of the Crawford Mountains at a likely spot to ford the Bear River the next day.

Wednesday, 14 August 1850.

august 14 we still go on but not founde the road yet   we think it is fifteen miles farther   we past some of the handsomest grass I ever saw in my life   we have now arrived at a place whare some one has camped   it seams like home here   we have a fare view of the wasatch mountains   they are completely covered with snow   it is a butifull sight in the morning when the sun shines on it

As they were heading south, the mountains she mentions are probably not the Wasatch, but the Uinta — the range branching to the east and perpendicular to the Wasatch. On a warm, slightly hazy September day, while traveling up the Bear River (south), the author noticed the Uinta Mountains came into view at latitude 41.57°N, or about five miles north of the current-day intersection of Highways 39 and 16. Sixteen miles travel puts the Davises west of the Bear River, three miles north of the Yellow Creek branch.

Sarah does not mention crossing the Bear River, which is unusual for Sarah who has been so careful about mentioning river crossings.

Thursday, 15 August 1850.

august 15 we have now arrived at the road and we travel vary fast   we have traveled ten miles and stoped to noon on yellow creek   not handsome at all   their has a come up her a man who wants to go with us to salt lake   he is sick with the mountain fever[49] and wants to ride in the wagon Elick has took him in   we have now arrived at eco creek a distance of twenty miles we have plenty of grass and good water

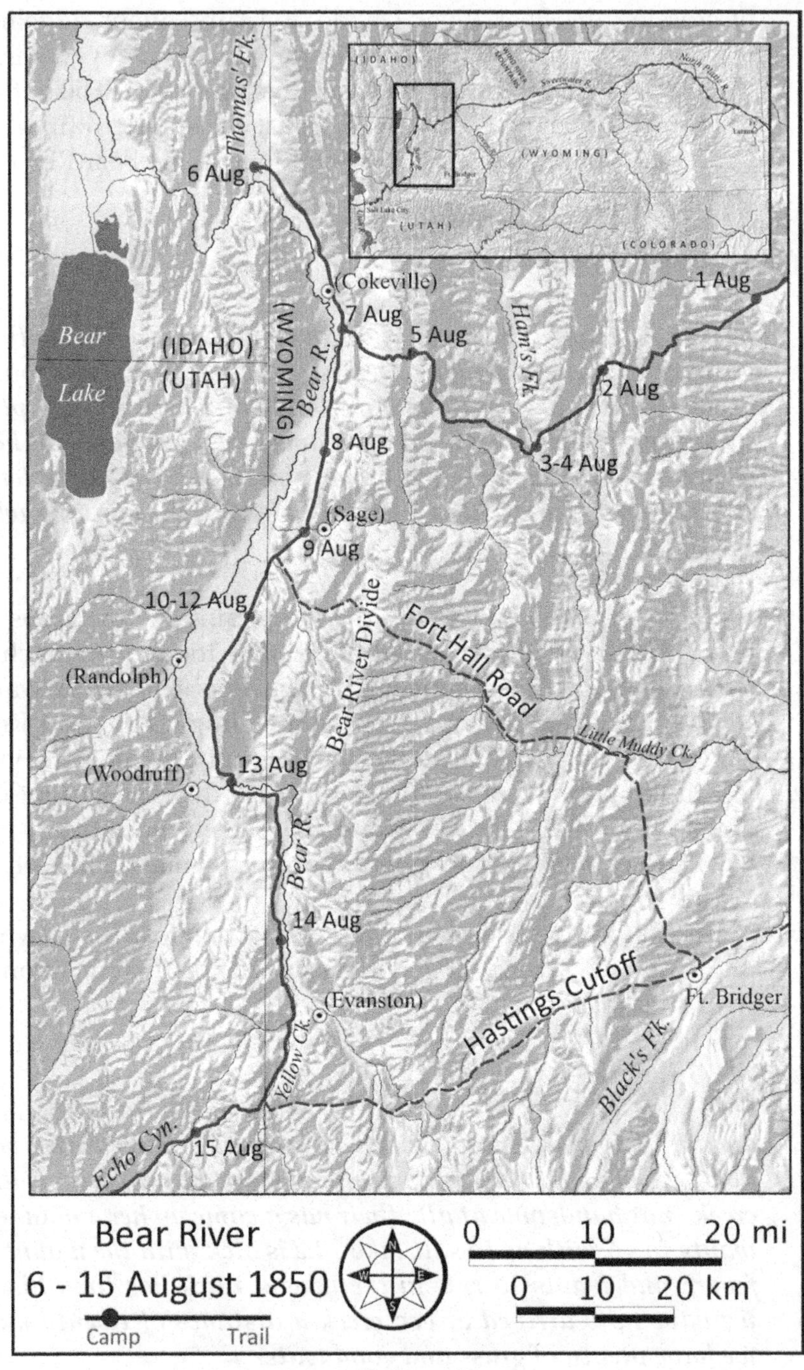

Map 17. Bear River.

After three miles they reached Yellow Creek and likely followed it south. After seven miles, they nooned along Yellow Creek's bank. Three more miles brought them to the Hastings Cutoff, then seven miles to a camp on Echo Creek.

Friday, 16 August 1850.

august 16 it is a vary bright clear morning   we now start vary early havin nothin to hinder us   we have now traveled now sixteen miles and stoped to noon on eco creek   we are opposite of a rock one thousand feete high [the stunning Echo Canyon] *we then went on to weber river and forded it and went one mile to camp whare thaeir was a good spring and plenty of grass weber river is a butifull stream about too rods wide and suift current and clear*

After descending Echo Canyon and turning north up the Weber River for a few miles, they camped on the western side of the Weber River near present-day Henefer, Utah. They traveled twenty-five miles this day, much of it downhill.

Saturday, 17 August 1850.

august 17 we started on in the morning and come to a warm salt spring we then past sevrel spring branches before comin to canion creek we come to canion creek then and crost it eleven times we nooned on canion creek whare their was one of the best springs I ever saw in my life we then went on some five or six miles and drove one mile up a canion in the mountain   it looks fright full here   [crossed out word: mosquito?] the valey is full of rocks of the largest kind

Sarah's description coincides with leaving the Weber River valley at current-day Henefer, Utah. They followed "Canyon Creek" up current-day "Main Canyon" then nooned around the summit, or Hogback Summit. They then followed Dixie Canyon down the west side of the summit before ascending Broad Hollow for one mile to camp. They traveled a tough eight miles this day.

Sunday, 18 August 1850.

> *august 18 we started on and traveled fivteen miles down hill*
> *all the way we then come to a large train some fifty men it we*
> *stoped to noon   it commenced to rain and it rained vary hard*
> *and haled some when it qit raining we went on   we had a vary*
> *harde time to git up on the mountain and still harder to git*
> *down when we got down we felt thankefull to think we ware*
> *safe   we camped on browns creek*

This day found the Davises crossing "Big Mountain" (Figure 15).[50] From base of East Canyon, the Davises traveled four and one-quarter miles and climbed 1,400 feet to reach its summit. They then descended almost 1,200 feet over two miles ("...harder to git down...") to reach Brown's Creek. Rain and intermittent hail accompanied their day's efforts.

Figure 15. Photo looking west from the top of "Big Mountain." *"we had a vary harde time to git up on the mountain and still harder to git down"* (Camera location: 40.8274°N 111.6541°W facing southwest.)

Monday, 19 August 1850.

> *august 19 their uer* [our or were] *catle ran a way   we thought teheir was no yuse in gardin them and all went to bed and the wolfs came and drove them of and killed one of the best cous we thought they had bin stolen from us   in the morning the men to lok for them and founde them ablut five miles off   we then set out for the salt lake valey and Elicks wagon turned over in the mud but still we reached the valey*

Twelve miles found them near the mouth of Emigration Canyon.

Tuesday, 20 August 1850.

> *august 02* [20] *we past through the city of the Great salt lake it is a polesent place here and seams to be improving with great rapidity   it seams to have a great deal of vegiatation to sell and some stores*[51] [In the diary, this word looks like sores, but upon closer examination there is a faint "t" placed above and between the "s" and "o."] *here we crost the utaw* [Utah[52]] *river and stoped it is vary suift curent and bout too rods wide*

Their location, after traveling eight miles through the Salt Lake valley, is across the Utah or current-day Jordan River.

The Holmes transcription of Sarah's diary places the Davises' location on 20 August on the Weber River.[53] A close examination of Sarah's 20 August entry, however, shows a not so clear but very readable, "u-t-a-w" (Figure 16). For a comparison, Sarah references the Weber River on 16 August (Figure 17). Here, the spelled out w-e-b-e-r is clear (though Sarah's "w" can look like a "u").

The Utah River is the name of the river flowing north from Utah Lake and draining into the Great Salt Lake. "Utah R." appears on period maps,[54] and various sources mark this "Utah River" as synonymous with today's Jordan River.[55] By whichever name, this river is on the western side of Salt Lake City very much as Sarah describes, "we past through the city of the Great salt lake…crost the utaw river and stoped…." A measured distance from the mouth of today's Emigration Canyon (where they spent the previous night) to the Jordan River along the Hastings Cutoff is about seven miles.

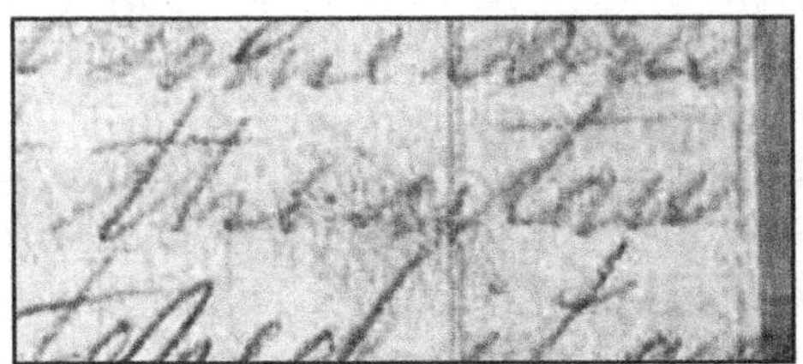

Figure 16. Sarah's description of the river where they camped on 20 August, "the utaw" the next line below is the word "river." (Yale Collection of Western Americana, Beinecke Rare Book and Manuscript Library.)

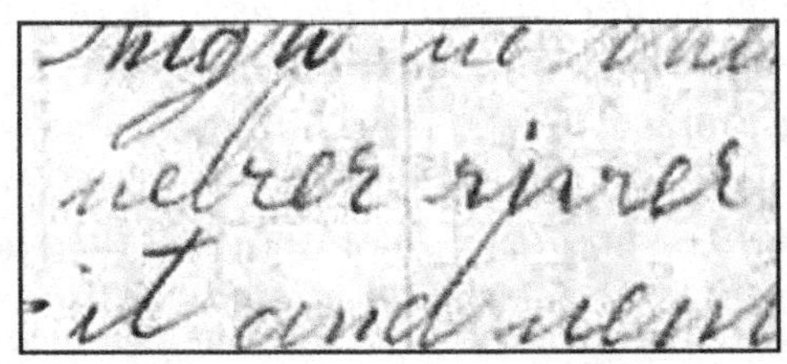

Figure 17. Sarah's writing of the word "weber" on 16 August. (Yale Collection of Western Americana, Beinecke Rare Book and Manuscript Library.)

If, on the other hand, we assume this is in fact the Weber River, then the Davises would have left Emigration Canyon, passed through Salt Lake City, and then turned north along the Salt Lake Cutoff to reach it—a measured distance of forty miles and impractical for a single day's journey.

Therefore, considering the text of the diary, period maps, period and current writings, and the distances involved to reach either the Jordan or Weber Rivers, it is clear that on 20 August the Davises "passed through the city of the Great Salt Lake...," crossed the current-day Jordan River, and then established a camp on the Jordan River where they stayed for the next two days, departing on the morning of 23 August 1850.[56] This is an important distinction; for if they were, in fact, at the Weber River, such a location would indicate a northern trek out of Salt Lake City vice a western trek. This could lead some to reasonably conclude the Davises took the Salt Lake Cutoff around the northern banks of the Great Salt Lake to reach the Humboldt River.[57] They did not take the Salt Lake Cutoff; they remained on the Hastings Cutoff as they entered the Great Basin.[58]

Figure 18. The "utaw river" (Jordan River) with the Oquirrh Mountains in the distance. This is a few miles south of where the Davises crossed. Where they crossed is now heavily built up. (Camera location: 40.7107°N 111.9233°W facing west.)

Wednesday, 21 August 1850.

august 21 we lay here

Thursday, 22 August 1850.

august 22 we lay here half the day and concluded to go to calaforna

There is no change from the 20 August location.

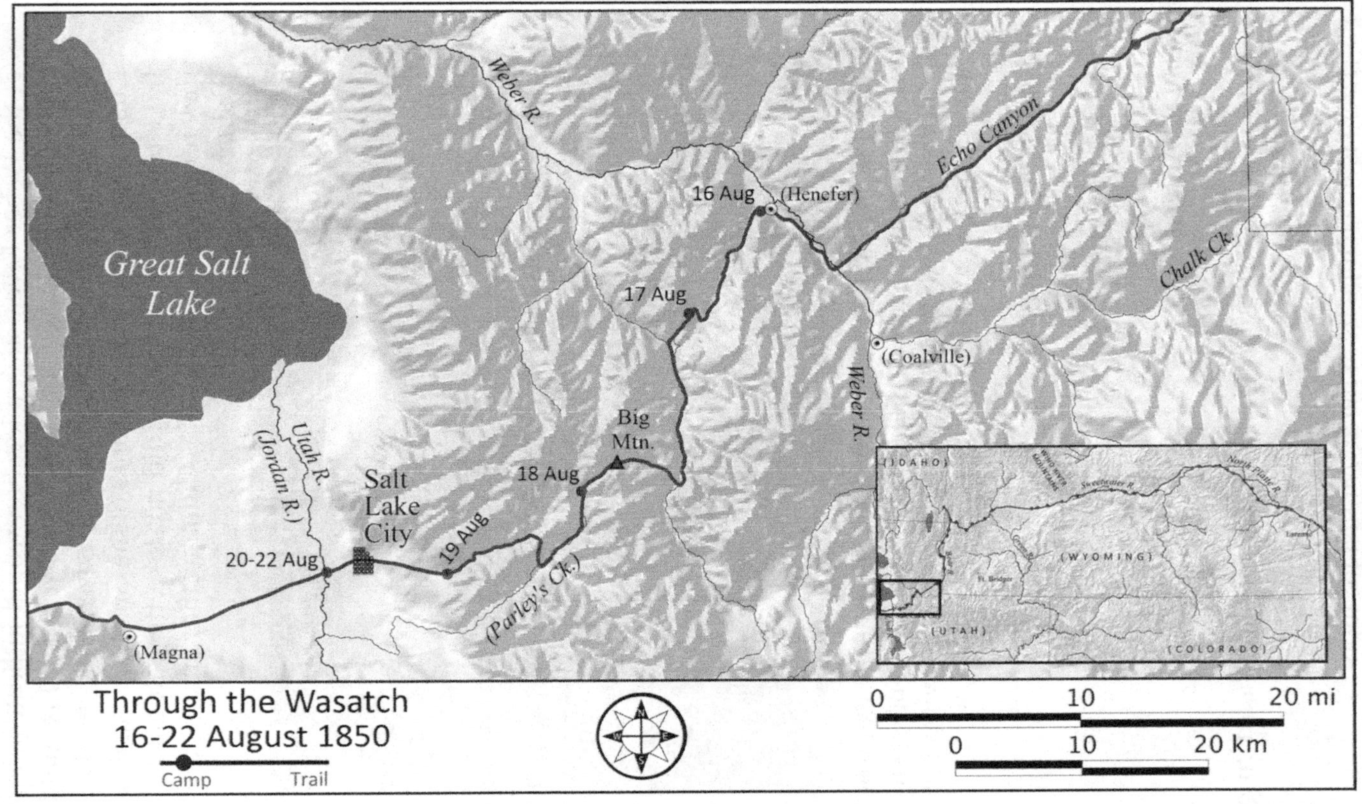

Map 18. Through the Wasatch.

Notes

[1] Keith Meldahl, *Hard Road West: History and Geology Along the Gold Rush Trail* (Chicago, IL: University of Chicago Press, 2007), 78n2. These foothills of the Laramie Range are "Black Hills" due to their dark stands of spruce and cedar.

[2] There are several different variations of the names of these rivers. Since most of these rivers are named for the early trappers in the area, the possessive is used. The 1846 Preuss map (section V) is used as a guide for the naming of these Wyoming Rivers.

[3] The author presents an argument for this route after Sarah's 9 August diary entry.

[4] John Steele, *Across the Plains in 1850* (Chicago, IL: Printed for the Caxton Club, 1930), 101. The author would have thought such a navigation mistake unlikely, if not impossible; yet, Steele warns against making the mistake, so perhaps grand errors of navigation like this occurred with greater frequency.

[5] Joseph Cain, "Letter of Joseph Cain," Deseret News (Salt Lake City, UT, October 5, 1850).

[6] Hubert Howe Bancroft, *History of the Pacific States of North America* (San Francisco, CA: The History Company, Publishers, 1889), 21:328.

[7] Ware, 3; Davis, "Diary of Sarah Davis," 8 October entry.

[8] Michael E. Mann, "Little Ice Age," ed. Michael D. MacCracken and John S. Perry, Encyclopedia of Global Environmental Change (Chichester: Wiley, 2002), 4.

[9] William Clayton, *The Latter-Day Saints' Emigrants' Guide* (St. Louis, MO: Republican Steam Power Press, Chambers & Knapp, 1848), 12.

[10] Franzwa, 46.

[11] Charles Preuss, "Topographical Map of the Road from Missouri to Oregon, Commencing at the Mouth of the Kansas in the Missouri River and Ending at the Mouth of the Walla-Wallah in the Columbia," Topographical (Baltimore: E. Weber & Co, 1846), Section III.

[12] Kenneth L. Holmes, *Covered Wagon Women: Diaries and Letters from the Western Trails, 1850*, Bison Book Ed. (Glendale, CA: A. H. Clark, 1983; reprint, Lincoln, University of Nebraska Press, 1995), 2:182. Dr. Holmes transcribes this "bufalo" as "antelope." Power transcribes it as buffalo. This script is very close to two other mentions of buffalo by Sarah (7 and 11 July) and very different from her script of "antelope" in her 13 August entry.

[13] Clayton, 13.

[14] Ibid.

[15] Preuss, "Topographical Map of the Road from Missouri to Oregon," Section III.

[16] Clayton, 13.

[17] Oxford English Dictionary, 2d ed., s.v. "recruitment."

[18] Clayton, 13.

[19] Ibid., 15.

[20] Charles W. Burdick, *The State of Wyoming: An Official Publication Containing Reliable Information Concerning the Resources of the State* (State of Wyoming, 1898), 85.

[21] Clayton, 15.

[22] Was this the Mr. John Steele who wrote *Across the Plains in 1850*? (Published initially as a serial in the Lodi Valley News in 1899, then in book form, printed by Caxton Club, Chicago, 1930.) While John Steele does not mention the Davises, he does mention the Estuses, a family also mentioned by Sarah as traveling companions. Since Mr. Steele mentions the Estuses but not the Davises, and Sarah mentions a Mr. Steele (Sarah is careful to only use a given name for family) as well as the Estuses, it is tempting to conclude that Sarah's Mr. Steele is John Steele, the writer. On the other hand, John Steele locates his whereabouts on 21 July as along the Sublette Trail at the Green River (ferrying emigrants across), having arrived at the Green on 17 July. Sarah and party arrived at the Green River on 31 July, two weeks later. Also, John Steele mentions encountering the Estus family on 22 July just west of the Green River; Sarah mentions a Mr. Estus and family in her diary, though they split company on 29 July at the Big Sandy (east of the Green). Therefore, unless John Steele or Sarah Davis made a significant error in dates, John Steele the writer was not the same "Mr. Steele" mentioned in Sarah's diary. Nevertheless, the fact that they are close in time and space, and they both wrote about their travels, is very helpful in describing conditions along this portion of the journey.

[23] Clayton, 15.

[24] The Davises traversed four significant "deserts" on their journey. The first after leaving present-day Casper, Wyoming; the second between the Big Sandy River and the Green River; the third, the sixty-seven miles between the Cedar Mountains and Pilot Peak; and the fourth, the famous "Forty-Mile Desert" between the Humboldt Sink and the Truckee River. The author does not attach this relatively short seventeen-mile desert to that list.

[25] This photograph was taken at a Bureau of Land Management interpretive plaque that reads, in part: "The Twin Mounds are a minor landmark along the Trail. These low hills on either side of the trail helped keep emigrants headed in the right direction on the final climb to South Pass."

[26] The author does not think Sarah is referring to Split Rock, which she would have passed, and did not mention, on the twentieth. Nor does the author think she is referring to the "twin mounds," which she mentions on the twenty-sixth. She may be referring to two ridges marking the ascent from the Sweetwater Valley to the higher Strawberry Valley area. Here, travelers climbed one ridgeline, followed by a short downhill descent into a small valley, then another climb up to the 7,200-foot level for a total climb of 550 feet over two and one-half miles.

[27] T. H. Jefferson, "Map of the Emigrant Road from Independence Mo. to St. Francisco California." Jefferson records seeing the Wind River Mountains from this same area. He also records the three Lewiston Lakes as "ponds."

[28] Clayton, 16.

[29] Andrew Child, *Overland Route to California* (Milwaukee: Daily Sentinel Steam Power Press, 1852; reprint, Los Angeles: N.A. Kovach, 1946), 26. Child calls these hills "Koin Mounds" and mentions a good spot to camp just past them.

[30] Steele, 99.

[31] Meldahl, 138.

[32] A summary of various authors' descriptions of the length of this desert is contained in a note by John Caughey in Ware, 26.

[33] Lavender, 77; Ware, 26n40.

[34] Clayton, 17.

[35] US Geological Survey, "Cokeville," Topographical (US Geological Survey, 1967); US Geological Survey, "Sublet," Topographical (US Geological Survey, 1985). The presence of "Mudy" River in Sarah's diary could well be evidence they took the Fort Bridger route. However, both a Mud Creek and a Muddy Creek appear along the Sublette Cutoff near where Sarah mentioned the "Mudy."

[36] These fellow travelers probably followed the Big Sandy southwest to reconnect with the Oregon-California Trail.

[37] Ware, 22.

[38] Fred Gowans and Eugene Campbell, *Fort Bridger, Island in the Wilderness* (Provo, UT: Brigham Young University Press, 1975), 44.

[39] US Naval Observatory, "Complete Sun and Moon Data for One Day: Locations Worldwide – Naval Oceanography Portal," 2011. That night the moon's disk was 65 percent full. Data used: latitude 42.5°N, 109.7°W, 30 July 1850, GMT-7.

[40] Oxford English Dictionary, 2d ed., s.v. "seine."

[41] US Bureau of Land Management, "US Department of the Interior Bureau of Land Management," 2011, http://www.blm.gov/wy/st/en/resources/public_room/gis/datagis.html.

[42] John. C. Frémont, *Memoirs of My Life*, 1st Cooper Square Press ed. (New York; [Lanham, MD]: Cooper Square Press; Distributed by National Book Network, 2001), 203.

[43] Ibid., 205–205.

[44] Ware, 27.

[45] Frémont, 203.

[46] Lavender, 77.

[47] Holmes, 2:269. From the 14 September 1850 diary of Lucena Parsons.

[48] Dale Lowell Morgan, *Jedediah Smith and the Opening of the West*, Second Bison ed. (Lincoln, NE: Bison Books, 1964), 237.

[49] Lavender, 71. An affliction that struck many pioneers traveling through the Wasatch Mountains. Lavender describes the symptoms as "... excruciating headaches and ... agonizing pains in [the] joints...."

[50] Clayton, 20.

[51] Bancroft, 21:300. The forces of supply and demand were not lost on the more permanent residents of Salt Lake City—prices of supplies needed by California-bound emigrants soared during the gold rush years.

[52] Charles Preuss, "Map of Oregon and Upper California from the Surveys of John Charles Frémont and Other Authorities," Topographical (Washington DC: US Senate, 1848).

[53] Holmes, 2:191.

[54] Preuss, "Map of Oregon and Upper California"; Jefferson, "Map of the Emigrant Road."

55 Heinrich Lienhard, *From St. Louis to Sutter's Fort, 1846*, trans. Erwin G. Gudde and Elisabeth K. Gudde, The American Exploration and Travel Series (Norman, OK: University of Oklahoma Press, 1961), 104n58; John P. McBride, "Pioneer Days in the Mountains," Tullidge's Quarterly Magazine, October 1883, 319, 320.

56 Davis, "Diary of Sarah Davis," 20 Aug entry; Sarah Davis, "Diary of Sarah Davis as transcribed by Minerva L. Power," note after 22 Aug entry. Minerva Power included a note which reads: "Grandma was much impressed by large streams of clear water that ran on both sides of the streets in Great Salt Lake City for many times has she told me about the beauty of the clear running water."

57 Robert J. Willoughby, *The Great Western Migration to the Gold Fields of California, 1849-1850* (Jefferson, NC: McFarland & Co., Inc., 2003), 196.

58 Bob Black, Linda Black, and Larry Schmidt, *Hastings Cutoff & Pack Trails Driving Guide* (Reno, NV: Trails West, Inc., 2010), 47, 71; Roy D. Tea, *The Hastings Cutoff: Grantsville to Donner Springs* (Salt Lake City, UT, 1996); Roy D. Tea, "Hastings Cutoff," telephone interview, November 29, 2011; US National Park Service, 268.

Chapter Four
The Great Basin

*we have past over some mountains to day for it is continually
mountain after mountain   now we have com in sight of a valey
it is some distance to it   we have now come to it   it is ten
miles a cross it to a butifull creek coming from the mountains*

Sarah Davis, 6 September 1850

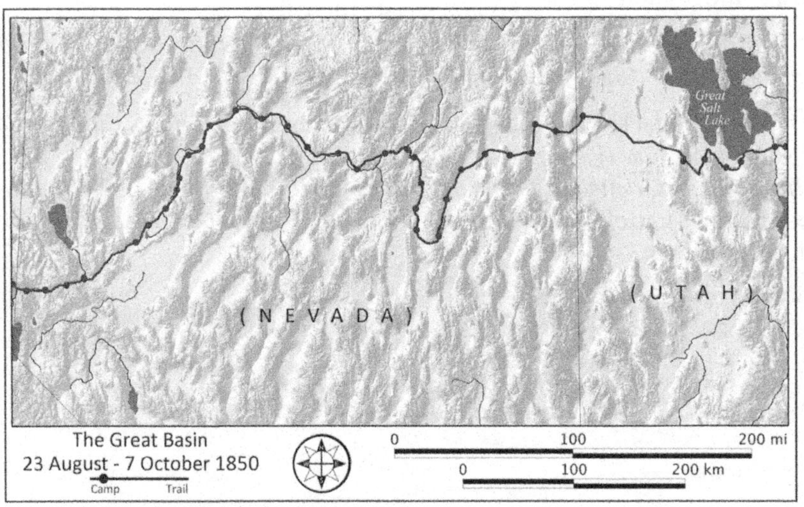

Map 19. The Davises' route across the Great Basin.

On 23 August 1850, after a two-night rest at the Utah (Jordan) River, the Davises started their traverse of the Great Basin. The Great Basin is a vast desert broken with dozens of significant, generally north-south mountain ranges, the collection of which Frémont described as "the teeth of a saw."[1] These ranges, however, do not present an impenetrable surface; there are gaps between them permitting westward travel. Where these gaps are inconvenient, a low saddle over a ridge will offer a feasible, though at times difficult, crossing.

They followed the Hastings Cutoff from Salt Lake City to the Humboldt River, a difficult cutoff that had doubtful advantage in terms of saving time and reducing distance and included a treacherous sixty-seven-mile stretch of waterless desert. Though some early explorers thought this route unsuitable for wagon and family travel,[2] Hastings

84

Cutoff would become a well used trail in 1849 and 1850. The Davises followed this cutoff from Salt Lake City to Pilot Peak, then twisted their way through the Great Basin ranges until crossing the southern end of the Humboldt River Mountains (Ruby Mountains).

Once across these mountains, the party renewed their familiar practice of following streams. They followed the small stream on the west side of the Humboldt River Mountains, today's Huntington Creek, north until it merged into the South Fork of the Humboldt River.

Here, along Huntington Creek, concerns about Native Americans began to dominate Sarah's diary; "...they surrounded us..."and "...we could see them skulkin evrywhare..." are typical entries. On more than one occasion, members of her party fired rifles to ward off the natives. This portion of the trail also plagued the Davises with dusty, sandy roads. A phrase like "...vary dusty all day" appears in just about every day's diary entry.

The South Fork soon brought the Davises to the Humboldt River west of current-day Elko, Nevada. At the Humboldt River, the Hastings Cutoff ends, and the Davises rejoined the westward flow of emigrants along the California Trail.

As difficult as this Hastings Cutoff route was (and still is), the splendor of the area was not lost on Sarah. Her diary is filled with phrases such as: "roars like a cataract...," "...perfect spring...," "...handsomest land I ever saw," "...clear as crystal...," and "...grass of the best kind..." to describe this beautiful, wild area.[3]

The Humboldt River reaches its end in the western part of the Great Basin. Then as today, as the river works its way west, it looses water to evaporation and the ground; the river's inputs are too small to keep up with the loss; consequently, the river just "sinks" into the desert floor—the Humboldt Sink. Past this point, travelers were faced with a forty-mile stretch of desert to the next reliable source of water, the Salmon Trout River (also called the Truckee River). This stretch of trail is the often-mentioned "Forty-Mile Desert." Although the Davises had crossed three significant "deserts" before, this "Forty-Mile Desert" was unique for its expanse of death and destruction. While crossing it, Sarah would encounter the remains of thousands of dead animals and almost a thousand human graves.[4] William Walker, who crossed this stretch in 1849, described the desert "...like a slaughter house strewed with dead animals, and the wrecks of wagons."[5] In her optimistic writing, Sarah only remarked "it is a sight to see the destruction of property here."

The Davises followed the Salmon Trout west until a few miles west of current-day Reno, Nevada, where they left the river and the Great Basin to ascend the foothills of the Sierra Nevada.

*   *   *

Friday, 23 August 1850.

> *august 23 we traveled fifteen miles and past plenty of salt   the lake is as salt as brine   let it be made as strong as it can be   the road is good here and plenty of good water we then come to a nother mormen setelment* ["E. T. Settlement" according to the Engloffstein map[6]] *it whare they was building a mill   a saw mill* [Benson's Mill] *we then went about a mile to the good springs caled bentons mill springs one was salt and the other not   we then camped being vary tired*

Their location, after traveling twenty-four miles, was near a stream about three-quarters of a mile south of Benson's Grist Mill. Sarah's assertion of a sawmill being constructed correlates closely with the description of this area given by Edward Tullidge in his "Histories," where he mentions the mill's construction in 1850 and subsequent use as a sawmill in 1851.[7] Fellow 1850 emigrant, Madison Berryman Moorman on 26 July encounters the same sawmill construction, "…some men were engaged in fitting some timbers for a sawmill."[8] The sawmill is also mentioned in a more recent newspaper article from 1997.[9]

Saturday, 24 August 1850.

> *august 24 we started on and come to salt works of the mormons we then went on to miles and stoped to noo*[n] *whare their was a salt spring   we then went on and come to a canebrake* [a field of canes[10]] *or grass grroin rather thick   this is caled willow creek   a good spring of fresh water   we stoped here to put up grass for our catle   a cross the desert their is plento of the best kind here for people that is a crosin the desert   we*[nt] *twenty miles to day*

Today, there are two Willow Creeks that cross Hastings Cutoff in this area, North Willow and South Willow Creeks. From their last location, a trip of twelve miles would place them along South Willow Creek, the first "canebrake" they came to. This location is in current-day Grantsville, Utah. Though they probably stopped here for the night, the distance between their previous day's camp and this location is just over half of Sarah's recorded distance; accordingly, they may have pushed on to North Willow Creek, or farther still, loading up with grass and pushing on past the creeks altogether.

Sunday, 25 August 1850.

> *august 25   we traveled twenty miles   we past more than tenty salt springs   the water loocked clear and as if it was the best water ever drinked   the one whare we nooned plased me the best   the water a bout five feet deepe and boiled up in evry direction* [possibly Burnt Spring]   *one place it boiled up had spouts as large as a as a* [she repeats herself from one line to the next] *man head and I thought of all kinds of beads   evry thaught of all color and sapes* [shapes]   *the blace biber* [blue bubbles, beads? (from the Power transcription)] *runin in evry direction*

This day the party would travel just over twenty-one miles. Leaving the Willow Creek area, they traveled northwest, rounded the northern point of the Stansbury Range, and then followed the west side of the Stansbury Mountains, Skull Valley, south. There are many springs coming off the Stansbury Range here. From north to south they are: Big Spring at the north point of the range; Burnt Spring, five miles from Big Spring; Mushrat (Muskrat) Spring, another two miles after Burnt Spring; Horseshoe Spring, two miles past Mushrat Spring; and finally a collection of springs fed by the Salt Mountain variously known as Hope Springs, Burnt Springs, or Elbow Springs.[11] From these last springs, emigrants would strike northwest twelve miles across Skull Valley for Redlum Springs.

Monday, 26 August 1850.

> *august 26 this morning it is raining   it seams so plesent to see it rain as we have not seen it rane since we came in the valey before   we now noon near a salt spring   we then went on to elbou spring   fresh water it is vary good to   we then* [went] *on tuelve miles farther to the mountain* [Cedar Mountains] *and found a spring* [Redlum Spring (now called Redlam)] *it is rather brackish but good water* [Stansbury and Gunnison in their 1851 map identified this spring as simply, "Brackish Spring."[12]] *we traveled nineteen miles to day*

Their location on this rainy day was Stansbury's "Brackish Spring," or Redlum Spring, along the east slope of the Cedar Range. They traveled twenty-two miles.

Tuesday, 27 August 1850.

> *august 27 we lay buy all day fixen for the desert   we start in the morning   our catle wer drove to miles to grass   the mountains here are vary high and some cedars groin on them and are vary rockey*

They remained at Redlum Spring another day to rest their cattle and generally prepare for crossing the desert to Pilot Peak.

Wednesday, 28 August 1850.

> *august 28 we have not started yet   have formed a new acquaintance with mrs crouch this morning   I think we will travel to gether to california gold digins*

> *august 28 we left the springs and started over the mountain and first thing we done to help us along was to turn over Elicks wagon   we were about one hour loading but nothing broke   we then on and had rufest road we have had atall* [This road is still rough; the author suffered a flat tire driving this same stretch in 2011.] *the distance ove*[r] *the mountain was five miles and it took us till night   we had to duble teams twice comin over and then it was vary harde drawin for the catle team yoke*

On the twenty-eighth they crossed (with some difficulty) Hastings Pass through the Cedar Mountains (Figure 19) and continued through the days and nights of the twenty-eighth and twenty-ninth across what historian Charles Kelley called "the most desolate stretch of desert in America," the Great Salt Desert.[13]

Figure 19. Hastings Pass in the Cedar Mountains. (Camera location: 40.7100°N 112.9281°W.)

Thursday, 29 August 1850.

august 29 this day it was vary hot and seams to me as if evry thing will perish we traveled all night of the twentieight and all night of the 29 buy this time I have got use to it alitle we have now crost the desert it apears to me as if this has bin a nother great salt lake [remarkably perceptive as this is the bottom of ancient Lake Bonneville[14]] *and I am all most ready to believe it is the gorunde is white with salt all over plenty of it we are now in sight of a mountain* [Pilot Peak]

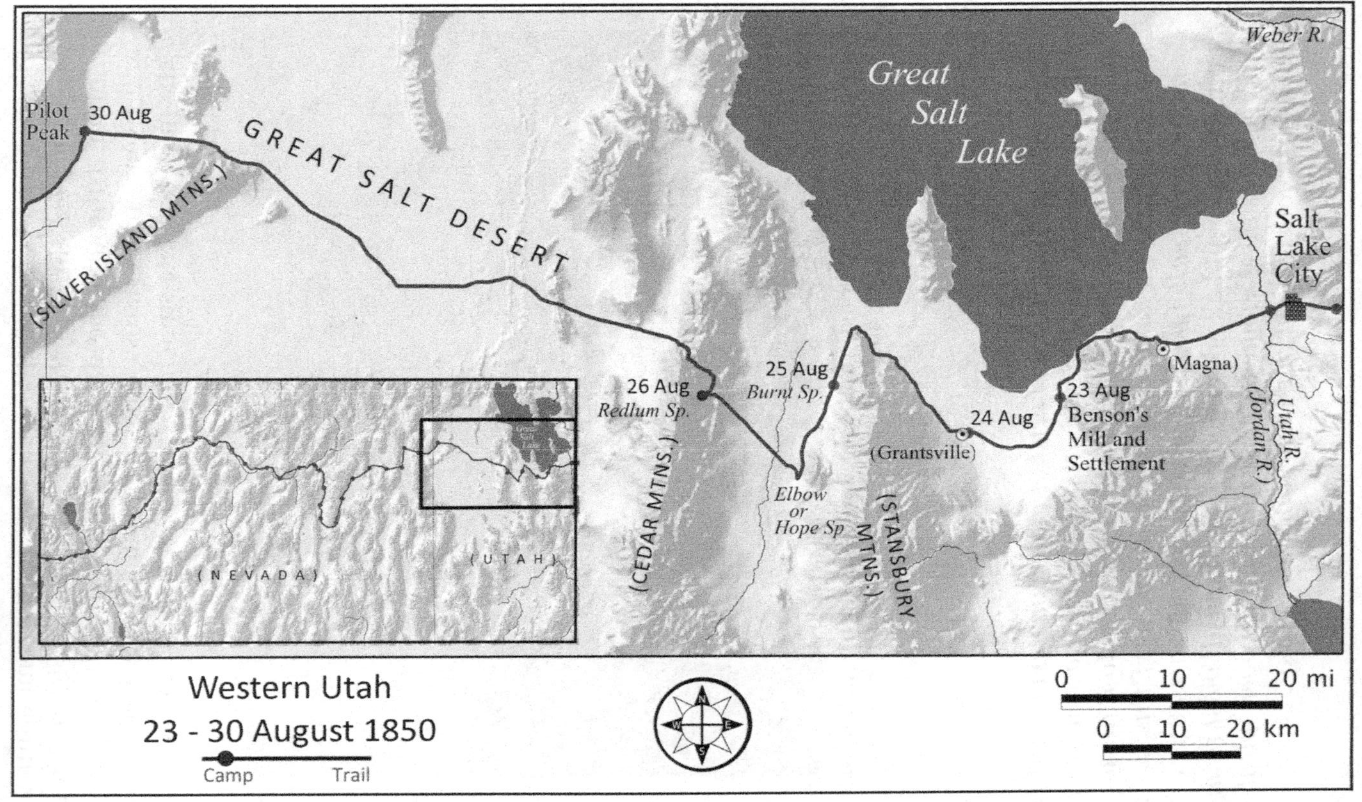

Map 20. Route between Salt Lake City and Pilot Peak.

Friday, 30 August 1850.

> *august 30 we raved* [arrived] *at land and water about eight o
> clock this morning we are a cross the great horn valey the
> men are all tired nearley to death as well as the catle the men
> are all a sleepe and the catle are a resting themselves we* [lost]
> *no catle nor horses* [Sarah's first mention of horses.] *we got
> through safe and are thankfull the Indians suarmed around
> us and are vary saucy it is vary hot today I think their was
> no one prished on the desert*

Their location after crossing the Great Salt Desert was at the
eastern base of Pilot Peak at Pilot Peak Creek (current-day
Donner Springs).[15] This part of the Hastings Cutoff was perhaps
the most difficult part of the entire journey. The sixty-seven miles
between Redlum Spring and Pilot Peak required three days and
two nights of travel through waterless desert.[16] Crossing this
desert without a water source and in the August heat, emigrants
would suffer greatly.[17] The Davises crossing was aided by fairly
high moon illumination on both nights.[18]

Saturday, 31 August 1850.

> *august 31 we left the desert spring with the intention of goin
> ten miles to grass and water and when we got their it was
> fifteen miles to grass and water we had a harde days travle
> some of our catle gave out they droped down in the dust*[19] *also
> became* [acquainted] *with a mrs slater from chicago today we
> traveled twenty five miles today and then founde no grass the
> men hunted round to find grass and founde it one mile*

After traveling just over twenty miles, the Davises camped just
east of today's Silverzone Pass.

Sunday, 1 September 1850.

> *september 1 sunday this morning is vary colde but the sun is up
> and clear we are here right in a large canion scarcely an inch
> of rume for the wagons to pass each other* [Silverzone Pass in

the Toano Range] *and vary ruff roads and rocky we starte on in a few minutes we have now started on and found grass in to miles and stopped to grasse our cattle we have vary dusty roads and have now traveled twelve miles*

They camped on this cold, clear, and dry day twelve miles west of Silverzone Pass at what the 1848 Preuss map describes as Whitton's Springs.[20] Sarah's description of Silverzone Pass is similar to Heinrich Lienhard's (another emigrant and author) description of a canyon with "high rocky ledges [on both sides]."[21]

Figure 20. Silverzone Pass. (Camera location: 40.9074°N 114.3031°W facing west.)

Monday, 2 September 1850.

september 2 we lay by all day on whiten spring and washed and grased our cattle we founde plenty of grass here

They remained at the springs. On this second day at these springs, Sarah records the name, "whiten spring." Both the Holmes and Power versions of Sarah's diary transcribe this as

"Whites" Spring. In Sarah's diary, however, the last letter (or two), written in pencil, of this word is squished in the crease along the spine of the diary — it could be "whites" or "whiten." Due to the proximity to Frémont's Whitton Spring, the author has transcribed this word as "whiten."[22] Though historians Korns and Morgan will later assign the name Whitten Spring to Mound Spring farther down the trail,[23] Irene D. Paden in her *Prairie Schooner Detours* will argue, citing geography, Frémont's recollections, the Moorman diary, and the Preuss map that current day "Big Springs" (previously known as the Johnson Ranch) is Whitton Springs, just as Sarah asserts.[24]

Figure 21. Hastings Cutoff leading to Flower Springs from Whitton Springs. (Camera location: 40.7777°N 114.5143°W facing south.)

Tuesday, 3 September 1850.

september 3 we started on and traveled eighteen miles to grass and water we found plenty of water here and some grass to day we have had good roads not vary dusty but some   we now take over the mountains for the humbolt river

Sixteen miles brought them to Flower Springs (also called Flowery Springs).

Wednesday, 4 September 1850.

september 4   we left some springs in large bogs and crost over the mountain [Flower Pass in the Pequop Mountains] * had vary dusty roads all day   we traveled about eighteen miles and came to water and grass   we have come to another chain of mountains and no humbolt yet   we camped here for the night we have good water here* [Mound Springs on the eastern slope of Spruce Mountain Ridge] * it is vary cold*

After traveling thirteen miles they would arrive and spend a cold night at Mound Springs.

Thursday, 5 September 1850.

september 5 we traveled some fifteen miles and got to a good camp ground plenty of good grass and water cold as ice   a butifull creak comin right from the mountains   it roars like a cataract and springs all round in every direction   our catle are giten fat on this grass I was vary sick all night here with a paine in my breast   their were three wagons come up last night with us I believe   here the mountain is all covered with snow

Their camp's location was on the east slope of the East Humboldt Range, almost sixteen miles west of their previous night's camp at Mound Spring. The National Park Service attributes this entry of Sarah's to Warm Springs, though both Sarah's party and the spring's water were cold.[25]

Friday, 6 September 1850.

september 6 we have past over some mountains to day [East Humboldt Range] *for it is continually mountain after mountain   now we have comin sight of a valey it is some distance to it   we have now come to it   it is ten miles a cross it to a butifull creek coming from the mountains   it is as clear as*

*cristal and cold as ice   we have traveled eighteen miles to day
plenty of grass of the best kind for catle*

This day's journey of almost seventeen miles brought the Davises to the eastern base of the Humboldt River Mountains (Ruby Mountains), possibly near current-day Thomas Creek.

Figure 22. A "T-rail" inscribed with Sarah's 5 September entry at Warm Springs. The Pequop Mountains are in the background. (Camera location: 40.7270°N 115.0300°W facing east.)

Saturday, 7 September 1850.

*september 7 we past over some of the handsomest land I ever
saw in my life   the land was completely covered with a thick
coat of grass   it looks like a perfect meadow   we passed some
five or six boiling springs   the smoke arose from them great fire*
[current-day Millers Hot Spring] *we passed more than twenty
springs of the best kind   we traveled twenty miles today and
traveled very late   we camped in a butifull place a stream on
each side*

They traveled south for nineteen miles before halting to camp for the night. They remained on the eastern slope of the Humboldt River Range.

Sunday, 8 September 1850.

september 8 sunday a butifull morning   the sun shines bright and clear as cristal   we have passed the most butifull sight I ever saw in my life   a perfect meadow with ten thousand springs in it a gushing right from the mountains   clear and cold some of them large anuf to cary any mill in operation   we have traveled twenty miles to day and stopped at foure oclock

Figure 23. The trail (road) over the Overland or Hastings Pass. (Camera location: 40.0183°N 115.5665°W facing west.)

Their location, after traveling south for almost twenty-two miles, was at the southern end of the Humboldt River Mountains near where Fort Ruby would later be established. There are several streams in the area.

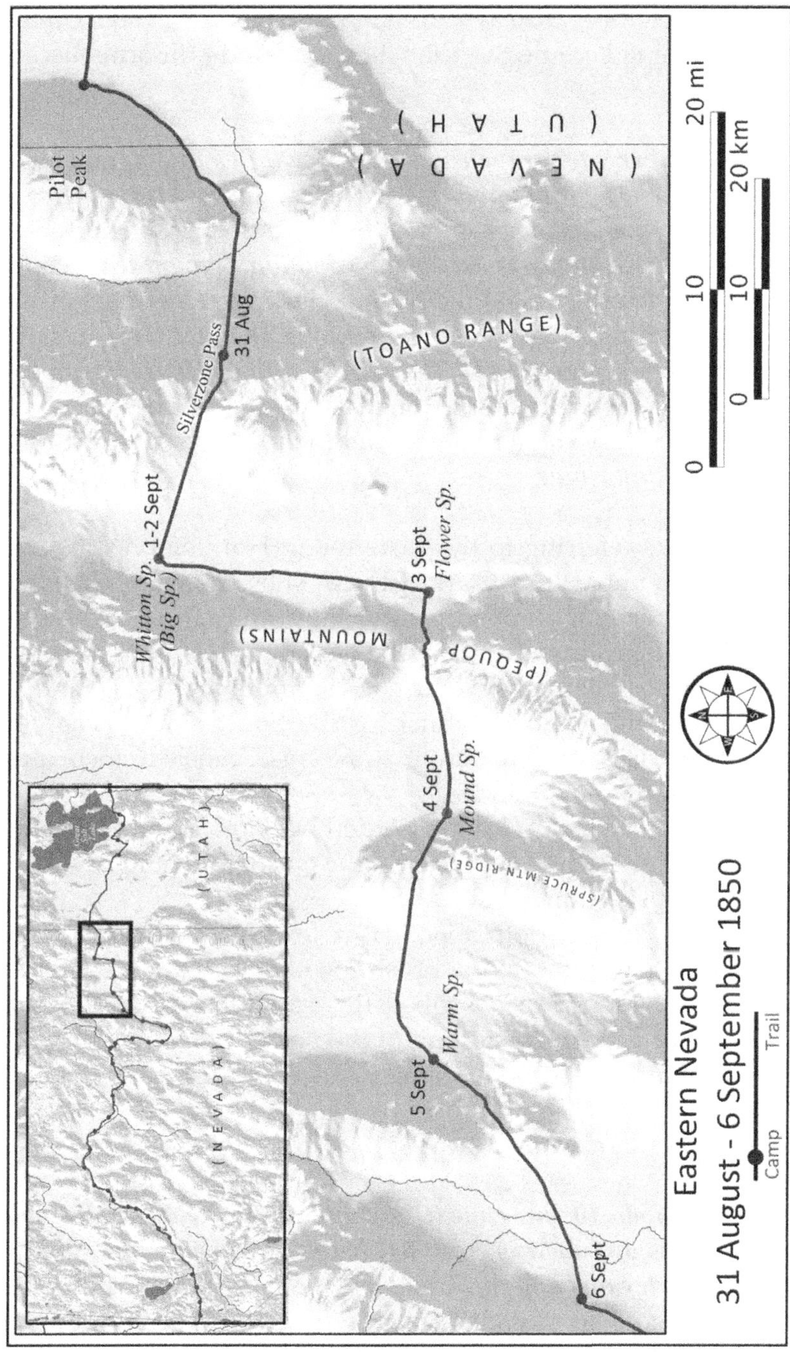

Map 21. Eastern Nevada.

Monday, 9 September 1850. On this day, current-day Nevada, Utah, and part of Wyoming became the Utah Territory, and California became a state.[26]

> *september 9 we traveled twenty five miles to day and came to clarks river   it is about foure feete wide and three feete deepe to day the dust was so bad that it was almost impossible to travel   we have passed over one humbolt mountain* [over what would later be called the second Hastings Pass and sometimes the Overland Pass] *and now come to another* [current-day Diamond Mountains]   *their are plenty of cedar here and some white pine or pitch pine* [She is speaking of trees in the pass.] *it looks very corse to me   and there is a curious fence which the Indians have*

Sarah is referring to the current-day Huntington Creek when she mentions the Clarks River. They came to this stream after traveling almost twenty miles and crossing the second "Hastings Pass" or today's Overland Pass. The stream she mentions has had several names: Smith's Creek, Huntington Creek, and Crane's Branch of the South Fork.[27] The closest (date-wise) name to Sarah's travels is Crane's Branch, a name given by Frémont in 1845.[28]

The low mileage recorded by Sarah could be due to the eight hundred-foot climb over the pass that would have slowed their speed somewhat.

The "curious fence" is a fence, or winnows, built by the natives by weaving brush together into a fence to channel game.[29] Moorman described this same fence's location about 300 yards past the summit of the pass.[30] Emigrants Bryant and Lienhard both describe similar fences in the area.[31]

Tuesday, 10 September 1850.

> *september 10 mr crouch had all of his team stolen by the Indians and their is truly left helpless   we lost one horse and mr porter one and mr Cromsley one   the indian tracks are all over here   we think their was a bout thirty here   we traveled about twenty five miles to get here and got in vary late   it was*

dark   the indians had a good time   we were all tired and were hungry and went to giten supper   they call this clarks river

This is the second entry for the same location. The previous day's entry seems to discuss the same journey and arriving at the same Clark's River. The calamitous events of the ninth may have precipitated a "lay over" to sort things out. This location also provided good water and grass for the cattle. On the other hand, with the hostile natives in the area, they may have pressed on to avoid further confrontation—making a second night in this location doubtful. Additionally, there is Sarah's comment about food, a comment that would have been written after a long day's journey (not a second entry), which would indicate more travels. That said, if they did travel another twenty-five miles on the tenth, then Sarah's diary accounts for too many miles between the Overland Pass and arriving at the Humboldt. A single twenty-five miles make her recorded distance more coincident with the actual distance traveled. On balance, therefore, it's more likely that this is a second journal entry for the same day.

Wednesday, 11 September 1850.

september 11 we traveled fifteen miles in a butifull valey all day   the grass is like a perfect meadow   the catle is giten fat here   we have still a vary dusty road   it almost suffocates us their is plenty of Indians signs here all the time   we still keepe in this valey all the time and dont no but we all ways will for their seems to be no hopes of giten out of here   we have now come to a sink of this creek entirely but we have founde a well

It is difficult to determine precisely the party's location at this juncture. However, since Sarah clearly fixes her position on 13 September at the eastern mouth of South Fork Canyon, one can backtrack to establish their location along the western slope of the Humboldt River Mountains, about twelve miles north of their previous day's location.

Sarah's comment about the stream reaching a "sink" in this area is interesting. The 1931 USGS map of this area, depicts

Huntington Creek (flowing north) turning from perennial to intermittent about fourteen miles south of current-day Jiggs, Nevada and remaining intermittent until just north of Jiggs, where it is charged by Smith Creek.[32] If the same conditions were present in 1850 as depicted on the 1931 USGS map, by late summer the intermittent stretch of the creek would be dry.

Figure 24. A small valley near the center of the South Fork Canyon. (Camera location: 40.7154°N 115.8314°W facing north.)

Thursday, 12 September 1850.

september 12 we traveled seventeen miles to day   we have passed one of the most butifull springs it comes right out of the bank and runs into the valey   it was vary dusty all day to day   we have now come in sight of a little creek and the most butifull grass I ever saw   the water is clear and runs swift   the stream is covred with willows and they look lovely

Their location was seventeen miles east of the mouth of South Fork Canyon and fifteen miles north of their previous day's camping location. Though Sarah does mention streams, there are several of them along this stretch, too many to make any firm conclusions as to which Sarah was referring.

Friday, 13 September 1850.

september 13   we traveled all day and only made seventeen miles   we passed some of the handsomest grass I ever saw in my life   we come to a nother creek it is splendid [South Fork of the Humboldt coming in from their right, or east]   *we traveled down it all the afternoon and at night we came to a canion which turned to the west   we have bin traveling north for to or three days   this stream gets larger here   their is plenty of fish in it but we have not caught any*

Their location was near the eastern mouth of current-day South Fork Canyon.

Sarah seems unsure of the number of days she had traveled on this side of the Humboldt River Mountains, commenting that it was either "...two or three days...." They crossed the Overland Pass on the ninth, laid over on the tenth, and started heading north up the valley on the eleventh — totaling three days of traveling north to get to this location.

Saturday, 14 September 1850.

We have traveled in this canion [South Fork of the Humboldt River] *all day and onley come ten miles   we have traveled in the creek half the time I believe or more and some of the banks ware vary steepe   the water is vary clear   we founde plenty of good wood here and grass in abundance and some fissh   we have now got out of the canion and camped*

Their location, after traveling almost twelve miles through this canyon (Figure 24), was the northern mouth of South Fork Canyon.

Sunday, 15 September 1850.

september 15 this day we traveled seventeen miles   this morning we come in sight of the northern road and some teams came up with us   this morning we met a vary large train comin in from the golde digins they were mormns comin to salt lake[33]   *we have now come to the humbolte river and the water is blood warme here and very clear*

This evening, after traveling almost seventeen miles, found them near current-day Carlin, Nevada. The northern road mentioned by Sarah is the main California Trail descending from the northeast. It was here they learned of California becoming a state on 9 September 1850.[34]

Monday, 16 September 1850.

september 16 monday we traveled twenty miles to day over ruff and rockey roads and we come to the river again [at Gravelly Ford] *this travel was vary dusty and harde on the catle   one of them droped down in the yoke suficated with dust   we have now overtaken a great many people and almost evry one of them out of provisions of any kinde   we solde almost fifty dolars worth of bakin*[35] *last night*

Their location, after traveling just over nineteen miles, was the southern point of the Emigrant Canyon, Gravelly Ford, located east of current-day Beowawe, Nevada. This location is based on distances traveled; Sarah's description of the Emigrant Canyon's rough road; and meeting the river again, presumably at Gravelly Ford. There, they remained on the northern bank of the Humboldt; there is no evidence they crossed the ford to the other side of the Humboldt. In fact, there is evidence that they did not cross. In the next day's entry Sarah mentioned, "we traveled seventeen miles and came to the river again," which would indicate that they headed away from the river, up the current-day Bluff Trail.[36]

Tuesday, 17 September 1850.

september 17 this day we traveled seventeen miles and have come to the river again   the Indians are vary thick the they have killed to men to day and took their ammunition and

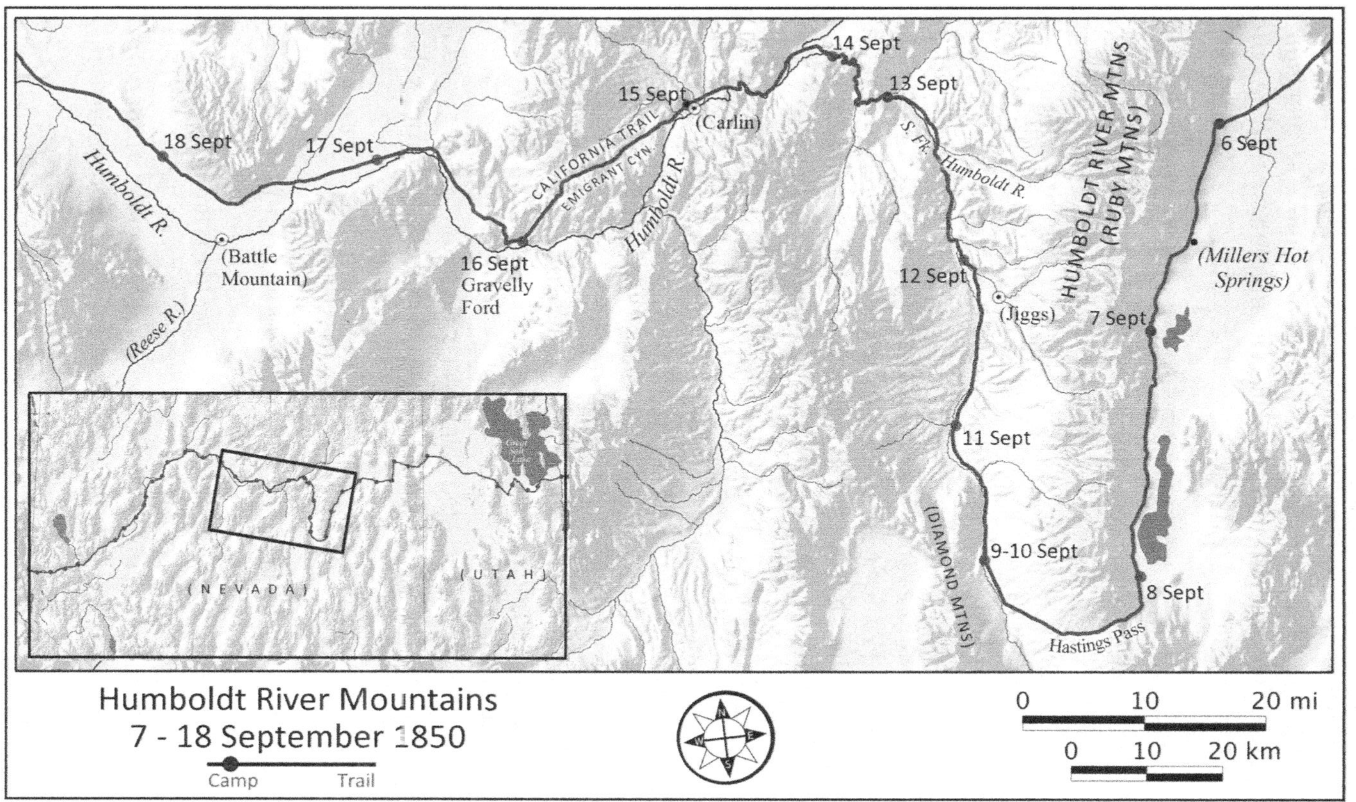

Map 22. Humboldt River (Ruby) Mountains.

horses and left them for the buzards   they devour them like we would sweete cake we have to have out a strong guarde all the time or we would be killed and may be we will be killed yet we dont no

This day found them heading over the low hills from Gravelly Ford, then northwest down the Humboldt River valley, today's Whirlwind Valley. As they rounded Shoshone point, now heading west again, they were confronted with a decision as the trail splits into three different paths: the most commonly used Northside Trail, on the north side of the Humboldt; the lesser-used Southside Trail, on the south side of the Humboldt; and the Wet Weather Route, also on the north side of the Humboldt.[37]

While Sarah does not directly mention which route they took, she also does not mention a river crossing after leaving Gravelly Ford, and since they were on the north side of the river at Gravelly Ford, it is reasonable to conclude they took the more common Northside Trail. However, if conditions warranted, they may have taken the Wet Weather Route, though there is no evidence of any significant local weather causing them to take the Wet Weather Route. On the other hand, since 1850 was a very wet year in the Humboldt Valley, they may have taken the Wet Weather Route after all.[38] If they did, then their path would arc to the north, rejoining the Northside Trail east of current-day Battle Mountain.[39]

They traveled just over seventeen miles this day and found a camping location just west of today's Dunphy, Nevada.

Wednesday, 18 September 1850.

september 18 this day is vary clear and bright   we have traveled twenty miles and to day noon we thought we ware all agoing to be devoured with Indians   they surrounded us   we thought therrie was too or three hundred   we coulde not tell exactly how many their was but we could see them skulkin evrywhare in the grass   mr hemingway shot one or suposed he did

Their location was twenty miles northwest from their last.

Thursday, 19 September 1850.

> *september 19 this morning is vary clear and bright   this day
> we have traveled seventeen miles to day noon we had the best
> grass I ever saw   it looked like a perfect wheate field   we then
> went on alittle ways and came to the river   their we found a
> man that had bin killed by the Indians and his heart taken out
> he was bried yesterday and their lay a dead Indian   it apears he
> was alone and the Indians came upon him and he shot one and
> then they shot him   he was founde with four arous shot in his
> breast and the Indian founde shot under the arm*

Their location was seventeen miles northwest from their previous day's camp.

Friday, 20 September 1850.

> *september 20 saturday* [Sarah's day of the week is off by one as
> the twentieth was a Friday.] *this day we traveled twenty miles
> and crost the river at noon   we founde good campin grounde to
> we camped on the oposite of the river from the other wagons
> we had plenty of good grass here   we had vary dusty roads to
> day   it was salaratus dust* [bicarbonate of potash, an ingredient
> in baking powder[40]] *there is plenty of salaratus here and plenty
> of lie* [lye] *to*

Their evening camp location was near the southern mouth of today's Emigrant Canyon where the trail rejoins the river after crossing Edna Hill. Here, emigrants found "considerable feed" for their cattle.[41] (There are two Emigrant Canyons. The first is between Carlin and Gravelly Ford; the second, the one mentioned here, is northeast of current-day Golconda, Nevada.)

There are two locations where it was common to cross the Humboldt in this area. The first is located just to the west of the current-day railroad siding, "Red House," and the second is located in Emigrant Canyon, a mile and a half northeast of today's Highway 789 crossing of the Humboldt.[42] Based on the distance from their last camping spot and the time of day of their crossing (noon), it is reasonable to assume they crossed at the first crossing point. Of course, it is probably an even bet on

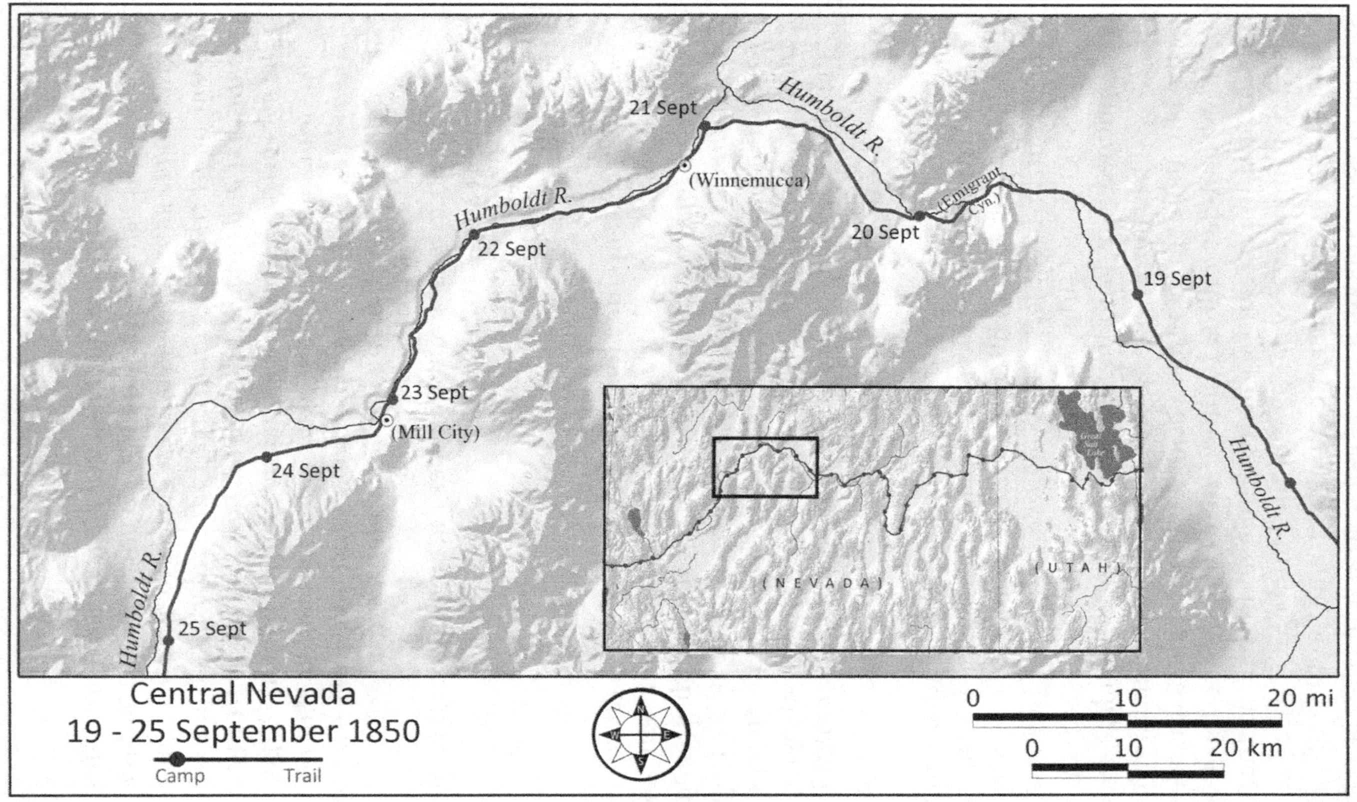

Map 23. Central Nevada.

which of the crossings they took, as it is difficult to gain a firm fix on several of their previous days' locations.

After leaving this Emigrant Canyon there were two general routes emigrants could follow to Big Meadows, the "Northside" or the "Southside." The Northside Trail followed the north bank of the Humboldt through a marshy area know as "Lassen Meadows" (current-day Rye Patch reservoir) then south to Big Meadows. The Southside Trail followed the southern bank of the Humboldt to Big Meadows, bypassing Lassen Meadows.

Since Sarah was on the north side of the Humboldt at Gravelly Ford, and she recorded crossing the river at the head of the second Emigrant Canyon on the twentieth, we can conclude that the Davis party was on Southside Trail as they left this Emigrant Canyon. Had Sarah continued along the Southside Trail, the time and distance measurements to Big Meadows correspond well with Sarah's recorded days and distances. Furthermore, Sarah's descriptions of graves and trail conditions fit well with other emigrant's descriptions of the Southside Trail.

Therefore, while it is possible the Davises crossed back over the Humboldt and followed the Northside Trail through Lassen Meadows (her description of a "low spot" in the river seems to suggest they did), it is more likely they made their way to Big Meadows along the Southside Trail.

Saturday, 21 September 1850.

september 21 this day it is vary colde day and cloudy and some rain ocasionaly   we have traveled twenty miles to day   we founde an advertisemnt to be carefull or the Indians woulde kill us   their is plenty of them here   we have plenty of good grass to day for the catle   we have now arived at camp   it is marshey grounde here with here and their a bead [bed] of saler-atus and a pond of alekelie   butifull green grass for the catle

Their location on this cold, overcast day was the camping area just to the northeast of current-day Winnemucca, Nevada, the Upper Meadows camping area.[43] They traveled just over seventeen miles this day.

Sunday, 22 September 1850.

> *september 22 we have traveled twenty miles to day and have vary good roads all except some sandy roads we had   we have now stoped to noon and I founde some of the handsomest flowers here I have saw In my life   their are plenty of ducks and sage hens here   we have had some of them and they are vary good   now we have arived at camp grounde it seems pleasant to stop   plenty of grass*

Following the Southside Trail, they pitched their camp about fifteen miles miles southwest of Winnemucca.

Monday, 23 September 1850.

> *september 23 monday* [She is back on track with the day of the week.] *this day we traveled twenty miles and founde good grass and good camp grounde   we coulde here the Indians a talking on the other side of river but we coulde not see them at all but could here them here   we had some sage hens and thought they ware a great rarity   it is vary colde and it has bin vary dusty all day   we have passed to or thre graves to day*

Their camping location on this cold fall day was thirteen miles from their last camping spot along the river near current-day Mill City, Nevada. In 1852, another emigrant, R. H. P. Snodgrass, will describe the graves of those buried in "'49, '50 and '51'" in this area.[44]

Tuesday, 24 September 1850.

> *september 24 tuesday this day we only traveled ten miles   the road being sandy and vary dusty and it was vary harde drawing all day*

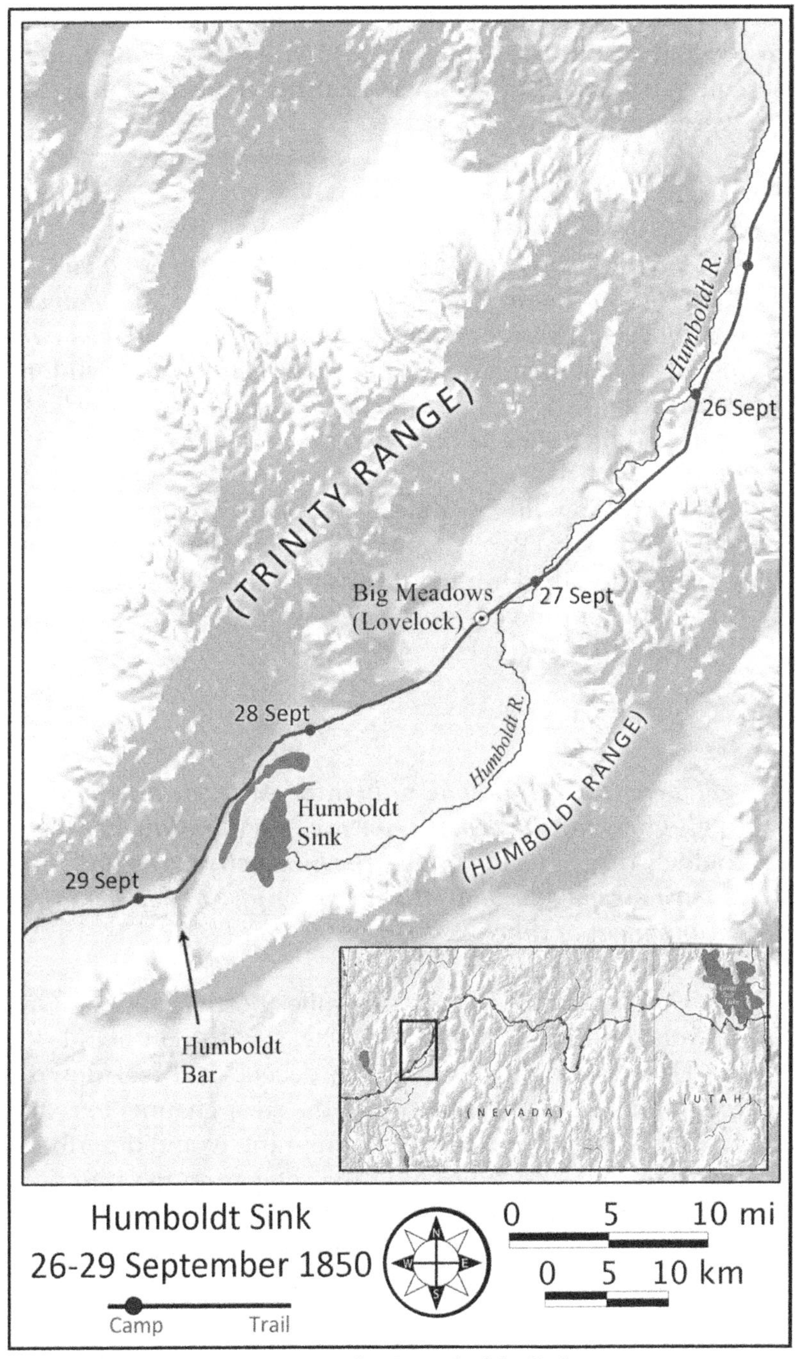

Map 24. The Humboldt Sink.

Traveling away from the river now, the Davises camped about ten miles south of Mill City. Julia Newton Wood, an 1853 emigrant, would also remark that the roads in this area were "very sandy."[45]

Wednesday, 25 September 1850.

september 25   this day we traveled fifteen miles and had a vary good roads all day   we had no dust at all   we camped in a low place on the river   their is a nother train camped clost by last night and the Indians thought they have a good c[h]ance to s[t]eal from them   as they came about [twelve[46]] oclock last night and they shot at them and they ran

After traveling fifteen miles, the Davises camped along the trail near today's Rye Patch travel center. Here, and for the next several miles, the Humboldt runs in a channel with high banks (150-200 feet) on each side. The Southside Trail follows along the top of the eastern bank.

Thursday, 26 September 1850.

september 26   this day we only traveled seven miles and stoped to git grass for the desert   we are in a vary lovely [this word could also be "lonely"] *place, the hills between us and the river is vary steepe and bad giten acros   just above here their an encampment of robers*[47]

The Davises camped about two miles north of today's Oreana, Nevada. From the Southside Trail (east of the Humboldt River), the Davises would have had to decend 200 feet down very rough and steep terrain to reach the river channel for water or grass. J. Robert Brown, an 1856 emigrant, would describe much the same experience reaching the river from the trail north of here, along similar terrain: "This bank is 150 feet high and is so steep that we could not get down with our wagons, and it is difficult even to get the cattle up and down..."[48]

Friiday, 27 September 1850.

> *september 27   this day we traveled fourteen miles the roads beeing vary dusty all day   we founde a good camp to night their is a wagon here that belonged to a nother train it seems they had a fight with the Indians seven days ago   their is plenty of good grass here and ducks in abundance here   the river here lays in sloughs* [a side channel of a river[49]]   *we are now in the vicinity of the sink I believe   Elick killed a beaf* [beef] *here and solde it all out*

The twenty-seventh finds the Davises at Big Meadows, an important stop along the California Trail. Here, emigrants would load up with grass and provisions in preparation for crossing the "Forty-Mile Desert."

Saturday, 28 September 1850.

> *september 28   we traveled fourteen miles to day and did not a camp till after night   we did not have a vary good camp grounde for I believe their are more than fifty dead horse here but their is plenty of grass here and water and plenty of good wood   this eavining we can see smoke in every direction some are Indians and some are emigrants   we can see here a plenty of fires   this day was vary dusty all day*

The Davises camped fourteen miles southwest of their previous location.

Sunday, 29 September 1850.

> *september 29   we traveled eight miles in the morning   we met a man that told us their was plenty of flour ahead and meate and coffe[50]   we went on then about three miles and their we met a train just come in with plenty of provisions   here we saw some of the digers[51]   they look frightful and same of their wigwams there was five I think   some of them came out to the road and they were bare necked*

Their location was near the Humboldt Sink where the trail split; the Truckee Route continues west and the Carson Route toward the southwest. The Davises took the Truckee Route.

Because of the wet conditions of 1850, the Humboldt River lake may have extended past the Humboldt Bar requiring the Davises to travel farther, west of the Humboldt Bar, before they would "leave the Humboldt entirely," as Sarah mentions in her next day's entry.[52]

Figure 25. The Salmon Trout (Truckee) River by Wadsworth, Nevada. (Camera location: 39.6324°N 119.2840°W facing south.)

Monday, 30 September 1850.

september 30   this day we struck the mane desert and now we leave the humbolt in tirely   we traveled all night and part of the day   we stoped to rest a half our to a time   the roads being vary bad   it is a sight to see the destruction of property here

Tuesday, 1 October 1850.

october 1 this day we traveled all day and all night we came to the boiling spring [current-day Brady's Hot Springs] *it is the greatest curiosity I ever saw in my life it will boil one yard high to a time this morning we arived at salmon trout river* [Truckee River[53]] *at about seven o clock*

They started their traverse of the "Forty-Mile Desert" on the afternoon of 30 September and traveled through that night and the day and night of 1 October, arriving at the Salmon Trout River on the morning of 2 October.

There was little illumination from the moon these nights, so their nighttime travel would slow with frequent stops to keep the cattle close.[54] Traveling almost forty miles put them at the east side of the Salmon Trout River, just outside of current-day Wadsworth, Nevada.

Wednesday, 2 October 1850.

october 2 we lay by here all day and a washed

Thursday, 3 October 1850.

october 3 we crost over the river and went to the trading post and stoped and lay by all day

It seems they made a very short trip (less than a mile) to the other side of the river. The Davises, having lost cattle after pressing on the day after crossing the Great Salt Desert, may have decided to give their cattle another day's rest before pushing up the Truckee River Canyon.

Friday, 4 October 1850.

october 4 we traveled twelve miles

Their location was thirteen miles past Wadsworth about half of the way up the Truckee River Canyon.

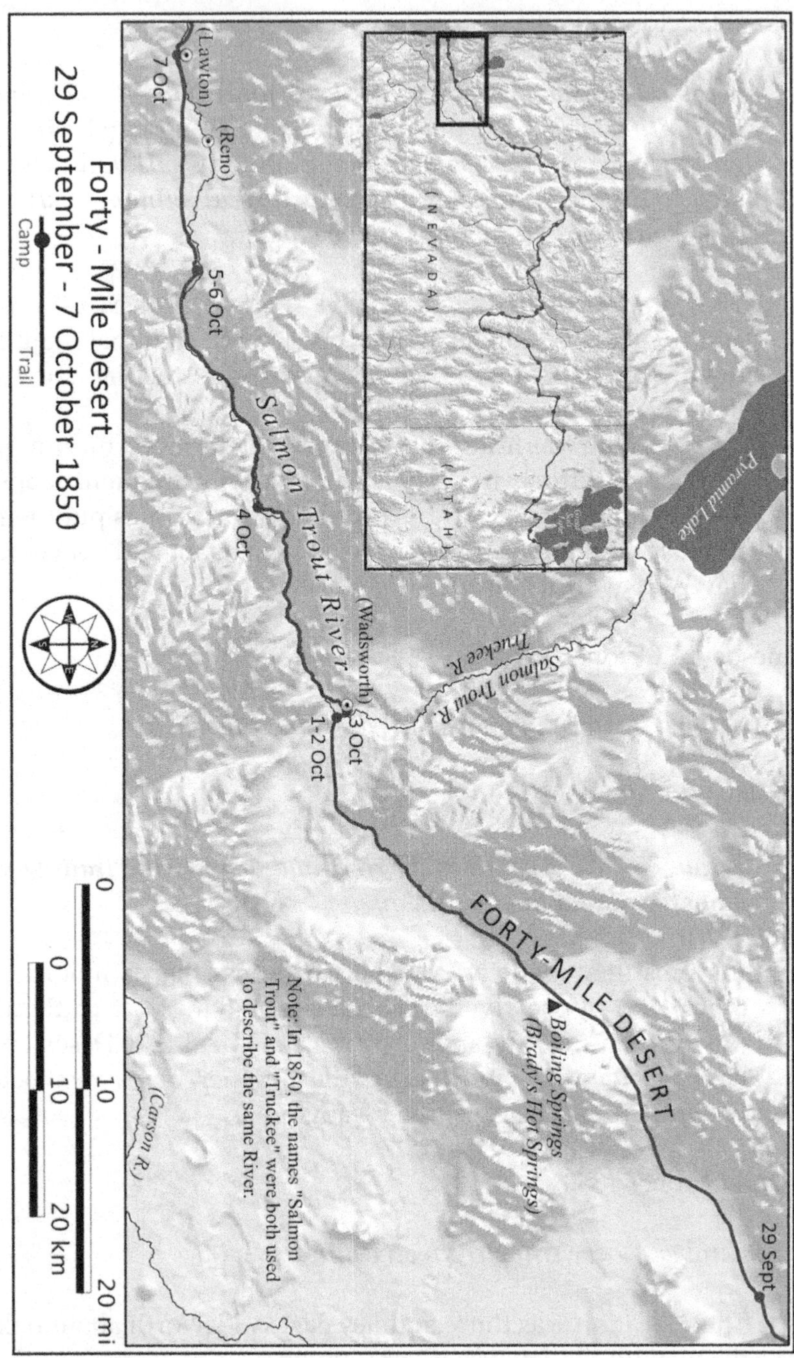

Map 25. The Forty-Mile Desert to the Sierra Nevada.

Saturday, 5 October 1850.

october 5 we traveled twelve miles

Their location, after an almost fourteen-mile journey, was at the top, or western end, of the Truckee River Canyon, just east of current-day Sparks, Nevada.

Sunday, 6 October 1850.

october 6   we lay by all day and fixed for packing

They remained at their 5 October camp preparing for the trip up and over the Sierra Nevada.

Monday, 7 October 1850.

we started on this morning and traveled twelve miles to the river   we had vary ruff roads all day   we have now come in sight of timber and now we have reached the river   we camped for the night   here is plenty of timber to be got for fires and plenty of good water and some grass for the catle

They camped along the Truckee River, twelve miles from their previous camp, near current-day Lawton, Nevada.

The next day, the eighth, they would begin their ascent of the Sierra Nevada.

Notes

¹ Frémont, 432.

² Bryant, 143.

³ Ibid., 191. Bryant provides the reader with some wonderful prose in his description of the beauty of these basins and ranges.

⁴ State of Nevada, "Carson River Chronology," n.d. This same information is found on state historical marker number 26.

⁵ William Z. Walker, "Diary of William Walker" (Provo, UT, 1949), 117.

⁶ F. W. Egloffstein, "From Great Salt Lake to the Humboldt Mountains. From Explorations and Surveys Made Under the Direction of the Hon. Jefferson Davis, Secretary of War by Capt. E. G. P. Beckwith, 3d. Artillery. E. [sic] W. Egloffstein, Topographer for the Route, 1855," Topographical (Washington DC: Selmar Siebert's Engraving & Printing Establishment, 1859).

⁷ Edward William Tullidge, *Tullidge's Histories* (Salt Lake City, UT: Press of the Juvenile Instructor, 1889), 2:99.

⁸ Moorman, 53.

⁹ Ray Boren, "Restored Site a Repository for Tooele's History," Deseret News (Salt Lake City, UT, September 18, 1997).

¹⁰ Oxford English Dictionary, 2d ed., s.v., "canebrake."

¹¹ US National Park Service, 35; Roy D. Tea, "Hastings Cutoff," telephone interview, November 29, 2011. Mr. Tea establishes Elbow Spring as synonymous with Hope Spring.

¹² Howard Stansbury and J.W. Gunnison, "Map of the Great Salt Lake and Adjacent Country in the Territory of Utah (Surveyed in 1849 and 1850)," Topographical (New York: Akerman Lith., 1851).

¹³ Ibid.; Egloffstein; G. M. Dodge, "Map of the Union Pacific Rail Road and Surveys of 1864, 65, 66, 67, 1868 from Missouri River to Humboldt Wells," Topographical (H. Lambach, 1869); Charles Kelley, *Salt Desert Trails:*

A History of the Hastings Cutoff and Other Early Trails Which Crossed the Great Salt Desert Seeking a Shorter Road to California (Salt Lake City, UT: Western Printing Co., 1930), 20, 22. The desert between the Cedar Mountains and Pilot Peak was known by various names. Stansbury labeled this desert simply "The Desert." Egloffstein followed suit on his 1855 map. The later railroad maps called this desert "The Great American Desert." Charles Kelley, in his 1930 book about the history of the Hastings Cutoff, Salt Desert Trails, calls this desert the "Great Salt Desert." The author will use Kelley's "Great Salt Desert."

[14] Grove Karl Gilbert, *Lake Bonneville* (Washington, DC: US Government, 1890), 20.

[15] Preuss, "Map of Oregon and Upper California from the Surveys of John Charles Frémont and Other Authorities."

[16] J. Roderic Korns and Dale Lowell Morgan, *West from Fort Bridger: The Pioneering of the Immigrant Trails Across Utah, 1846-1850* (Logan, UT: Utah State Historical Society, 1951; reprint, Logan, UT: Utah State University Press, 1994), 244. History records several distances between Redlum and Pilot Peak Springs, generally between forty and eighty miles. The author's "GoogleEarth" analysis produced a distance of sixty-eight and one-half miles. Roy D. Tea, applying decades of study and exploration of the Hastings Cutoff, calculates sixty-seven miles. The author differs to Tea's sixty-seven miles.

[17] Mary Lee Spence and Donald Jackson, eds., *The Expeditions of John Charles Frémont*, vol. II (Urbana, IL: University of Illinois Press, 1973), 44n12; Kelley, 116. Kelley in his *Salt Desert Trails*, Quotes an emigrant's (John Wood) description of the scene at Pilot Peak three weeks before Sarah arrived:

> "Emigrants arriving here all the time from the desert, almost famished for water; they say men, women and children are dying with thirst and fatigue…. Mr. Hall, who left his wife on the desert yesterday, is preparing to go back after his wife and wagon…. They [a rescue party of sorts] found many [fellow emigrants] at the point of death…"

[18] US Naval Observatory, "Complete Sun and Moon Data for One Day: Locations Worldwide — Naval Oceanography Portal." Data used: latitude 40.8°N, longitude 113.34°W, 28 and 29 August 1850, GMT-7.

[19] Frémont, 433. Frémont, while camped at Pilot Peak Springs, noted a requirement to allow animals to "resté" for multiple days after an arduous trek like crossing the Great Salt Desert. Because the Davises pressed on the very next day after reaching Pilot Peak, their animals may have suffered from lack of "resté."

[20] Preuss. "Map of Oregon and Upper California from the Surveys of John Charles Frémont and Other Authorities."

[21] Lienhard, 123.

[22] Frémont, 433.

[23] Korns and Morgan, 18. Here, Korns and Morgan present their logic establishing Whitton Spring as Mound Springs.

[24] Irene D. Paden, *Prairie Schooner Detours* (New York: The Macmillan Company, 1949), 95; US Geological Survey, "Feature Detail Report for: Big Springs," Geographic Names Information System, 2012, http://geonames. usgs.gov/pls/gnispublic; Frémont, 433. While both Paden and Moorman will spell the name of this spring "Whitten," it is properly "Whitton" after the name of one of Frémont's men.

[25] US National Park Service, 268.

[26] US Senate, Resolution Introduced by Senator Henry Clay in Relation to the Adjustment of All Existing Questions of Controversy Between the States Arising Out of the Institution of Slavery (The Compromise of 1850), January 29, 1850; Senate simple resolutions, motions and orders of the 31st Congress, ca. 03/1849-ca. 03/1851; record group 46; Records of the United States Senate, 1789-1990; National Archives, http://www.ourdocu-ments.gov/doc.php?doc=27.

[27] US Geological Survey, "Feature Detail Report for: Huntington Creek," Geographic Names Information System, 2011.

[28] Frémont, 434.

[29] Moorman, 121n145.

[30] Ibid., 63.

[31] Bryant, 188; Lienhard, 124. Bryant describes such a fence, constructed of cedar and interlaced with willow, while crossing the Toano Range in 1846. He later learned that natives built these fences to catch rabbit. Lienhard also describes such a fence, which he also later learned was used for catching antelope.

[32] US Geological Survey, "Jiggs Nevada" Topographical (U.S. Geological Survey, 1931).

[33] Kelley, 120; Joseph Cain, "Letter of Joseph Cain." This is the returning Joseph Cain party. Brigham Young sent this group of thirty-five to the California Gold Diggings in 1849. Meeting the Davises on 15 September, they then took the Salt Lake Cutoff to arrive in Salt Lake City on 2 October. Cain's letter provides insight on the conditions along the main California Trail.

[34] Davis, "Diary of Sarah Davis as Transcribed by Minerva L. Power." Note by Power; Richard K. Brock and Donald E. Buck, *A Guide to the California Trail Along the Humboldt River,* 2d ed. (Reno, NV: Trails West, Inc., 2007), 44. In this excellent guide, Mr. Buck places Sarah's location on the sixteenth in current-day Carlin after traveling across the Greenhorn Cutoff. While this makes sense based on the same geography described (the rocky roads and returning to the river), placing the Davises in Carlin after crossing the Greenhorn Cutoff on the sixteenth does not fit with the time and space, either past or future, of Sarah's narrative. Sarah's narrative places her in the Carlin area on the fifteenth, not the sixteenth.

After discussing other evidence with Mr. Buck (telephone conversation and email of 18 December 2012), he agrees with the author's assessment that the Davises did not take the Greenhorn and spent the night of the fifteenth in Carlin then made their way to the Gravelly Ford on the sixteenth.

[35] This word could be "baking" or "bacon." "Baking" makes more sense, as there is no mention of swine in the entirety of the diary.

[36] Brock and Buck, 63.

[37] Ibid., 66.

[38] Ware, xvi. In the Historical Introduction to Joseph Ware's book, John Caughey (who introduced and provided notes for Princeton's 1932 reprint of the 1849 edition) remarks, "He [Ware] did not anticipate...the Humboldt Valley's unusual wet season in 1850...."

[39] Brock and Buck, 63, 70.

[40] Oxford English Dictionary, 2d ed., s.v. "saleratus."

[41] T. J. Van Dorn, "The Diary of T. J. Van Dorn" (Yale Collection of Western Americana, Beinecke Rare Book and Manuscript Library, Yale University, 1849), quoted in Brock and Buck, 93. The August 13 diary entry of T.J. Van Dorn records "Considerable feed here...."

[42] Brock and Buck, 94.

[43] Ibid, 101.

[44] R. H. P. Snodgrass, "The Journal of R. H. P. Snodgrass" (Yale Collection of Western Americana, Beinecke Rare Book and Manuscript Library, Yale University, 1852), quoted in Brock and Buck, 119. "July 16. Coming down this stream we have seen the skulls of a number of persons who have been buried in '49, '50 & '51 and have been dug up by the wolves...."

[45] Julia Newton Wood, "Diary of Mrs. Julia Newton Wood 1853," accessed December 29, 2012, http://www.geckodance.com/oregontrail/diary1853.html. From her 18 August entry: "Roads some as they would be on the Humboldt; very sandy, dust blew very hard..."

[46] This time is difficult to discern in the diary. Powers reasons the time as "twelve" and Holmes to "tehn." Since Powers transcribed the journal decades before Holmes and from the original, the word was probably clearer and easier to read when she transcribed it. Accordingly, I've used "twelve."

[47] Holmes, 2:200; Davis, "Diary of Sarah Davis as Transcribed by Minerva L. Power," 26 September entry. The Holmes version reads: "...vary steepe and bad a wagon just broke here there is an encampment of robers." Powers transcribes this entry as: "... very steep and bad getting across. Just across here there is an emcampment of robbers."

[48] Robert J. Brown, *A Journal of a Trip Across the Plains of the U.S., from Missouri to California, in the Year 1856* (Columbus, [Ohio] The author. 1860), quoted in Brock and Buck, 136.

[49] Oxford English Dictionary, 2d ed., s.v. "slough."

[50] Brock and Buck, 149. Enterprising traders were loading wagons with provisions and traveling to this area to sell food and goods to the emigrants, many of whom were desperate.

[51] Frémont, 391; Bryant, 194. The Oxford English Dictionary is curiously quiet on the "digger"; Frémont, however, is not. In his recap of his second expedition to the West (1843-1844), Frémont describes the digger as "…humanity…in its lowest form….Dispersed in single families; without fire-arms; eating seeds and insects; digging roots (and hence their name).…" Bryant describes the "diggers" in the area around current-day Elko as "Soshonees."

[52] Brock and Buck, 155; Ware, xvi. Historical introduction by John Caughey.

[53] US Geological Survey, "Feature Detail Report for: Truckee River," Geographic Names Information System, 2011.

[54] US Naval Observatory, "Complete Sun and Moon Data for One Day: Locations Worldwide — Naval Oceanography Portal."Data used: 39.50 °N 119°W, 30 September 1850, GMT -8.

Chapter Five
The Sierra Nevada

*it is vary colde here and I am giting vary tired of my
journey   the mountains is covered with snow*

Sarah Davis, 10 October 1850

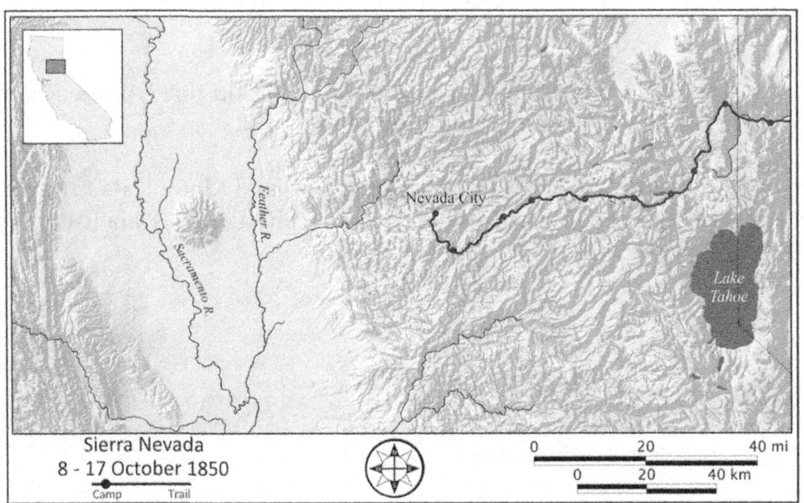

Map 26. The Davises' route across the Sierra Nevada.

A heavy snowstorm met the Davises as they headed up their first rocky, steep hill of the Sierra Nevada. After reaching the hill's summit, the northern shoulder of today's Verdi Range, they descended into Dog Valley, where they found a small stream and level ground for a camp. The next morning, they headed south along good roads through the basins of several heavily forested valleys until they reached today's Prosser Creek, where they stopped for the night.

The next day, they left Prosser Creek and traveled to Donner Lake's outlet stream, where they stopped to noon. Since it was too late to attempt a summit crossing and the weather was still poor, the Davises remained at this noon location for the night.

On the morning of 11 October, the Davises traveled up Coldstream Canyon and then crossed the crest of the Sierra Nevada over Roller Pass. Once over the pass, they traveled down the western slope for a short distance to camp at Summit Valley.

122

The Davises then followed the trail west as it paralleled the South Yuba River. At Crystal Lake, the South Yuba River veers northwest, and the trail then follows a small tributary of the American River until reaching Emigrant Gap. The Davises crossed Emigrant Gap and descended into Bear Valley. The Davises then climbed Lowell Hill Ridge and followed its crest, paralleling the Bear River, until they reached the Greenhorn Creek area, where they turned north and followed various mining trails until they "landed in Sierra Nevada City" in the afternoon of 17 October 1850.

*   *   *

Tuesday, 8 October 1850.

> *october 8   this day we crost the river* [the Salmon Trout River] *twice and then we came in to the timber   it is plenty   we now leave the salmon trout river and take over the mountain we have now come over the mountain to a valey* [Dog Valley] *whare their is grass for the catle and now we stop to feede   we have traveled seven miles   their is a small creek running here which answers for our use and for the catle   we have now a vary heavy snow storm   the mountain is white in the snow and it is vary cold here   I am almost frozen and the children   the men seem to stand it vary well*

Leaving their 7 October camp, the Davises crossed the bends of the Salmon Trout River and then climbed 1,200 feet up the rough, rocky trail that parallels today's South Branch of Dog Creek. Rounding the northern point of Verdi Range, the path opens into the small, pretty Dog Valley. They traveled eleven miles this day.

Wednesday, 9 October 1850.

> *october 9   we traveled fifteen miles   we have passed some of the handsomest pine trees I ever saw in my life   some of them five feete through and since we had vary handsome roads all day through some pleasant valeys of grass and a handsome creeke winding through the valey   plenty of grass to for the catle all arounde*

Fifteen miles south of Dog Valley put the Davises along Prosser Creek. Their camping site was probably under today's Prosser Reservoir. The "pleasant valeys" Sarah mentions are pleasant still; they are the Hoke Valley, some small valleys along the Little Truckee River, and the Russell Valley.

Figure 26. Dog Valley seen from the shoulder of Verdi Range. (Camera location: 39.5485°N 120.0442°W facing northwest.)

Thursday, 10 October 1850.

october 10 this day we traveled onley about seven miles   it a leven oclock when we have stoped to noon   we founde good grass here and plenty of water and wood   we cannot cross the sumit so we stop here till morning [Note: the Holmes version has this as "…we came to cross the sumit…"; both the Power version and the author read this date's diary entry as written here.] *their is plenty of good timber here and pitch pine   it is vary colde here and I am giting vary tired of my journey   the mountains is covered with snow*

Seven miles from their Prosser Creek camp put the Davises in the Truckee Valley, a half-mile east of today's Donner Lake near the intersection of Donner and Cold Creeks.

Figure 27. Cold Creek in Coldstream Canyon. (Camera location: 39.3148°N 120.2318°W facing west.)

Friday, 11 October 1850.

october 11 we have traveled eight miles to day   we crost siere nevada mountain it was vary steepe   we had to duble our teams to git up and then had a vary harde time we founde plenty of snow here and plenty timber and plenty rock a little more than we like   we have got over and found a bottom covered with grass and we founde a butifull creek here [the South Yuba River]

Three routes are commonly referenced as paths over the crest of the Sierra Nevada in this area west of Donner Lake: a northern route, Stephens Pass, which roughly follows today's Donner Summit road; a middle route, Coldstream Pass; and a southern route, Roller Pass.[1]

The route over Stephens Pass followed the northern bank of today's Donner Lake, then climbed over a steep, rocky, and very difficult pass to the north of today's Donner Peak.[2] If the Davises took the northern route, Sarah would have likely mentioned Donner Lake, the northern edge of which parallels this route for more than two miles; she did not. Moreover, since

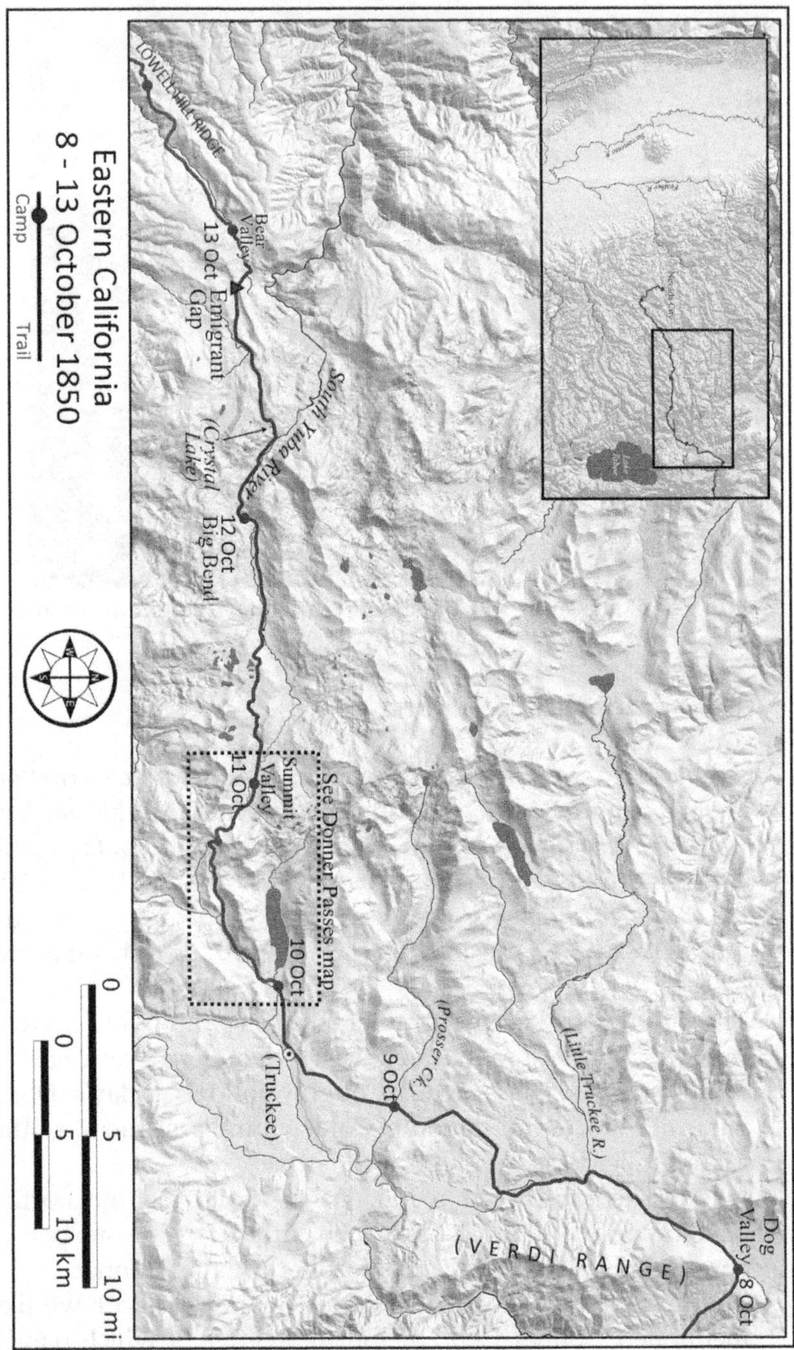

Map 27. Eastern California.

126

the northern route seems to have fallen out of use after 1847,[3] it is unlikely this was the route the Davises took.

The middle route followed Cold Creek on the south side of Schallenberger Ridge for several miles before turning north to cross the crest between Mount Judah and Donner Peak at Coldstream Pass. Once across the pass, this route descended to the west and then rounded Mary Lake on the way to Summit Valley. Since Sarah did not mention Mary Lake, and since there is some question if this pass was used by emigrants at all,[4] this route also seems an unlikely course for the Davises.

Roller Pass then becomes the more probable route taken. Roller Pass's extremely steep conditions required emigrants to gang their animals together, upwards of twenty yoke (forty oxen), at the top of the pass; a wagon at the base of the pass was connected to the oxen with a long chain. Logs were placed under and perpendicular to the chain at the crest of the summit; these logs, or "rollers," rolled under the chain acting as bearings to ease the pull.[5]

It was not long before emigrants discovered and improvised ways around the engineering requirements of Roller Pass.[6] In 1846, Heinrich Lienhard records that his party was able to cross Roller Pass by double-teaming their wagons and ascending immediately to the right from the base of Roller Pass.[7]

Since Sarah does not mention rolling logs, long chains, and enormous teams of oxen, she probably crossed by taking the path to the right of the base of the pass, just as Lienhard did.

As with most emigrants, the Davises found it necessary to camp at Summit Valley, the first level, grassy, and watered area after the crossing.

They traveled just over nine miles this day.

Saturday, 12 October 1850.

october 12   this day we traveled sixteen miles and came to yubar river [Yuba, but at the time, "Uber," according to Bryant[8]] *it covred with stones of all sizes and sorts from a hens ague to the size of a wagon   the water is clear and good   it about six feete wide   we have had the ruffest roads I have ever saw in my*

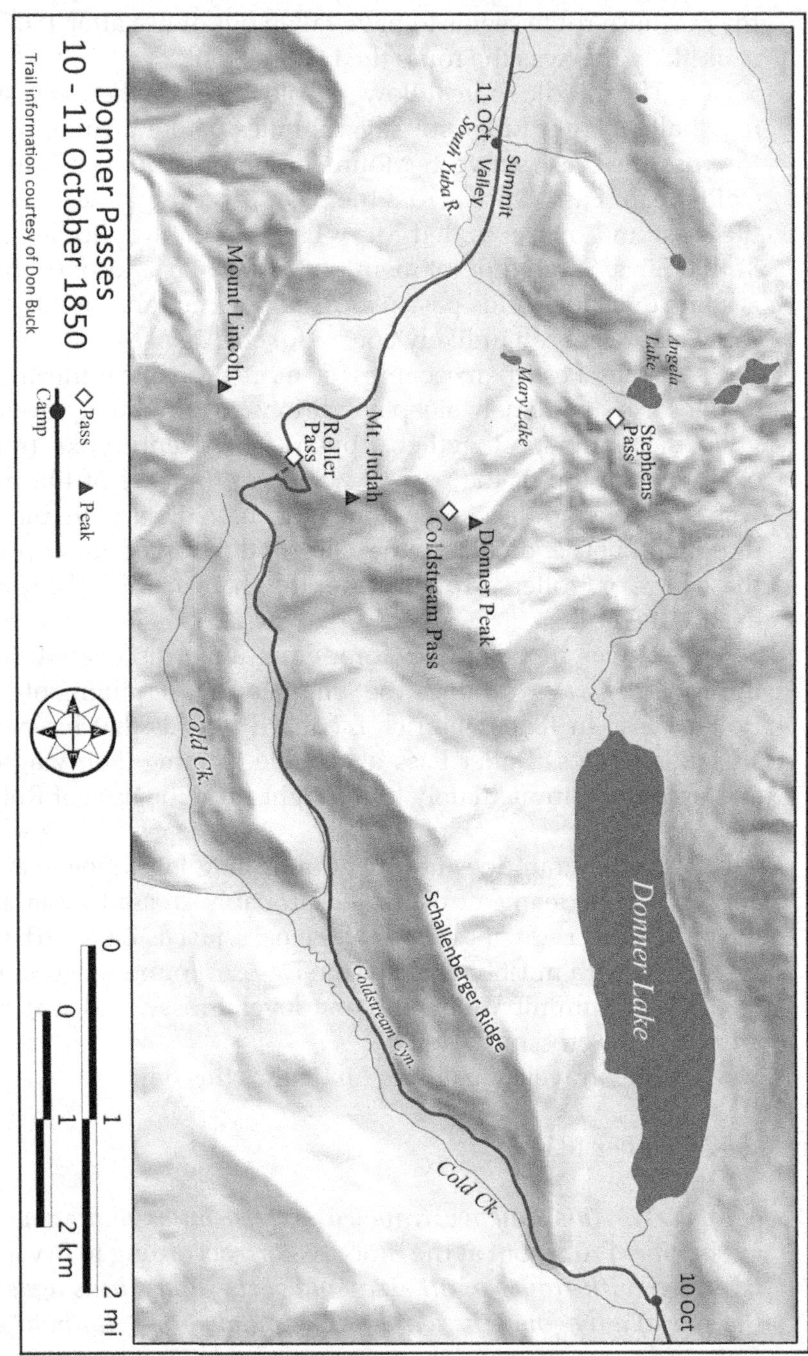

Map 28. Donner Passes.

life   some places were solid rock and it was butifull to see it we passed over a mountain of all sizes and sorts   we passed some handsome timber to day

Over the years, many fellow diarists echoed Sarah's assertion of rough roads. Irene D. Paden sums up these descriptions of this road in her *The Wake of the Prairie Schooner* as "Up and down—up and down on the mountain side the mules or oxen tugged the rumbling, lurching, tipping wagons, stopping every few feet to pant and blow."[9] Such inconveniences slowed the Davises and may have caused Sarah to overestimate her recorded distance. A distance of ten miles placed them in a camping area near today's "Big Bend" that matches her description.

Sunday, 13 October 1850.

october 13   this day we traveled onley twelve miles and had vary ruff roads all day   we past one trading post to day   we have past to or three lakes to day   we also passed one cedar tree which measured ten feete and I think their might have bin ten catle taken off   we now come to some grass for the catle and camp

Continuing west, the Davises traveled three miles before the South Yuba River turned north and away from the trail near Crystal Lake. After several miles, they crossed Emigrant Gap and made the steep descent to Bear Valley. They continued about a mile to the western edge of the valley where they camped for the night. They traveled eleven miles this day.

The mention of a trading post is not surprising. By 1850, supply, demand, and the profit motive produced a small industry of trading posts, many of them mobile, along the trails over the Sierra Nevada.[10]

Monday, 14 October 1850.

october 14   this day we lay buy all most all day and now we have started on   we come to a hill which is a mile up and a mile down[11] and now we stop grasse our cattle and now it is raining frost and snowing in the mountain   there is plenty wood here to for fires   plenty of oak

Leaving Bear Valley, the trail splits. The main Truckee Route continues west along the Bear River; the other route, the Nevada City route, heads up Lowell Hill Ridge to Washington Ridge, the crest of which is followed, more or less, all the way to Nevada City. Sarah's party could have taken either route in 1850, but her comment of 16 October (two days after leaving Bear Valley), "we lay by all day in bear valey…," indicates that they were still paralleling the Bear River and not on the Washington Ridge.[12] Therefore, they left Bear Valley and followed the Truckee Route to the Greenhorn Creek area, where they struck north to Nevada City.[13]

After spending most of the day in Bear Valley, they headed west along the Bear River for about four miles before ascending Lowell Hill Ridge, which they then followed southwest before camping at or near Deadmans Flat.[14] This was a short traveling day for the Davises; they traveled just under seven miles.

Tuesday, 15 October 1850.

October 15   we traveled twelve miles and had vary good roads all day

They spent the morning following the crest of Lowell Hill Ridge until noon when they descended its very steep northern slope to Steephollow Creek. They nooned here before ascending the ridgeline to the north, which they followed west for about five miles before stopping close to the Bear River near Greenhorn Creek, which was sometimes called "Bear River."[15]

They were in mining country by this point, as both Steephollow Creek and Greenhorn Creek were populated with miners.[16] This day they traveled almost fourteen miles.

Wednesday, 16 October 1850.

october 16   we lay by all day in bear valey to grasse our catle

Here, camped near Greenhorn Creek, they were only about ten miles from Nevada City. The cattle were probably quite tired, so another day here was prudent. Also, since it is doubtful they knew of Nevada City's existence when they left Kingston, they probably used this extra day to send one or two of the brothers on horseback to Nevada City as an "advance party" to size up the town.

Figure 28. Bear Valley viewed from Emigrant Gap. (Camera Location: 39.2992°N 120.6725°W facing west.)

Thursday, 17 October 1850.

october 17   we landed in siera nevady city and it is city to this making five months since we left home

They left their camp in the Greenhorn Creek area and traveled northwest, following streams and mining trails over and around low hills to a large grassy valley, today's Grass Valley. From here, they turned northeast and crossed through a low gap on a small ridgeline to the Deer Creek valley and Nevada City. Once in Nevada City, they spent the night of the seventeenth camped just north of town by today's Sugarloaf Mountain.[17]

131

Friday, 18 October 1850.

> *october 18   we got under shelter with mr potinger   he had a house partly finished   it is a sight to see the miners here*

Saturday, 19 October 1850.

> *october 19   we lay in mr potingers for the* [The diary ends.]

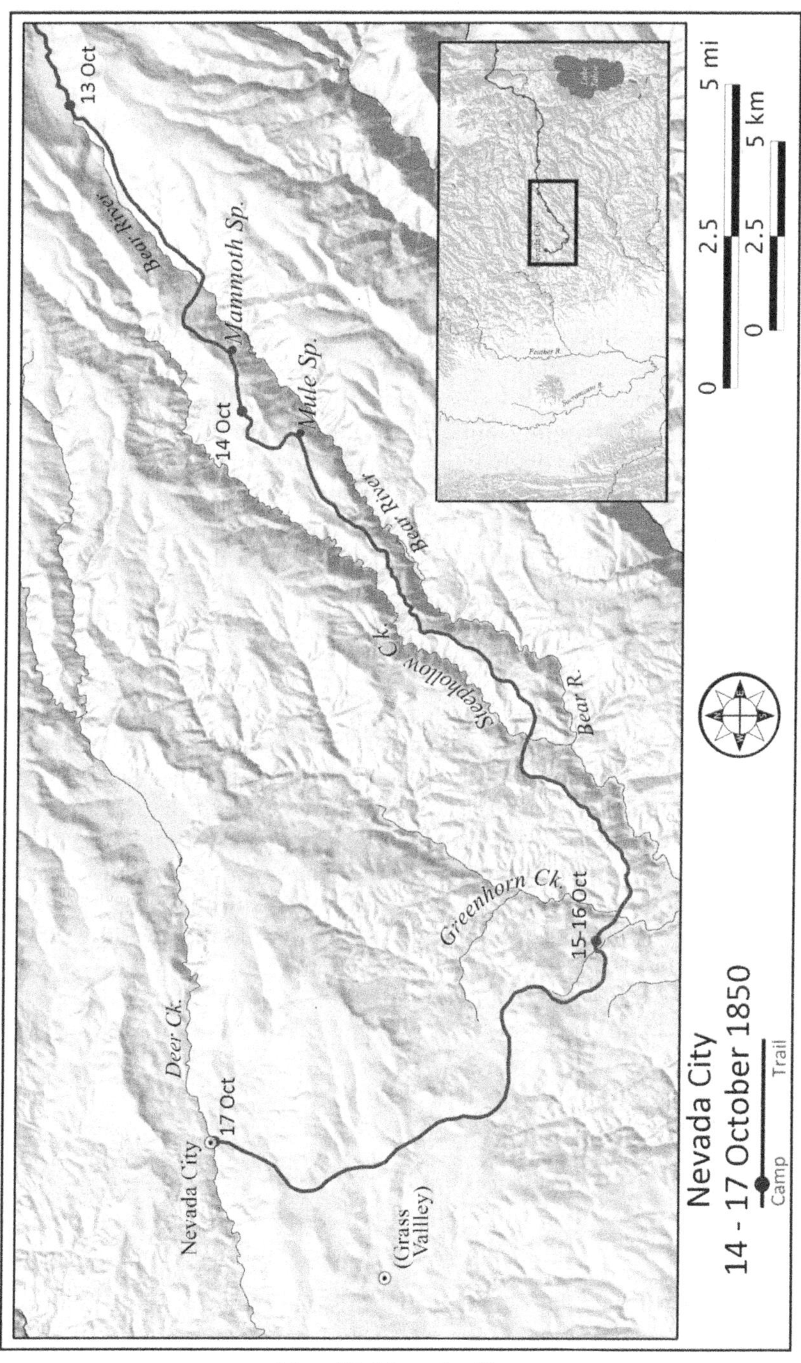

Map 29. Nevada City.

Notes

¹ Olive Newell, *Tail of the Elephant: The Emigrant Experience on the Truckee Route of the California Trail 1844-1852* (Nevada City, CA: Nevada County Historical Society, 1997), 172, 174-175.

² Ibid., 172.

³ Ibid., 179.

⁴ In conversation and correspondence with trail historian Donald (Don) Buck (December 2012), he pointed out that the research conducted by Donald Wiggins in the 1990s convincingly casts doubt on Coldstream Pass ever being used by emigrants. He and others contend that the evidence points to emigrants exclusively using what became known as Roller Pass, beginning in the late summer of 1846. On the other hand, Olive Newell in her *Tail of the Elephant* (pp. 196-202), offers evidence suggesting emigrants did cross Coldstream Pass. As explained here, I don't think Sarah crossed at Coldstream Pass.

⁵ Meldahl, 257.

⁶ Don Buck points out that there are two routes over Roller Pass. The earliest one ascended directly from a small meadow below the saddle between Mount Judah and Mount Lincoln. Here, emigrants had to use log rollers to pull their wagons to the pass. Because of the difficulty in making this very steep direct ascent, emigrants quickly found a somewhat easier way to ascend Roller Pass by opening a slanting wagon route from the meadow to the right that got them to a ledge just below the summit ridge, where they turned left along the ledge for about 1,000 feet to the saddle. Both of these routes over Roller Pass required emigrants to hitch up as many yoke of oxen or mules as possible to make it to the top.

⁷ Lienhard, 175.

⁸ Bryant, 232.

⁹ Paden, *The Wake of the Prairie Schooner*, 467.

¹⁰ Unruh, 275.

¹¹ The author acknowledges that this description, a mile up and another down, then followed by grass for grazing, sounds suspiciously like crossing Emigrant Gap and then spending the night in Bear Valley, as many

emigrants did. However, had the Davises spent the night of the fourteenth in Bear Valley, then they only had the fifteenth to travel the twenty-one miles to reach "the bear [river] valley…" (Greenhorn Creek), where they spent the night of the fifteenth and sixteenth, a feat that seems unlikely considering Sarah's recorded distance of twelve miles on the fifteenth as well as the rough trail conditions. Perhaps Sarah recorded the climb and descent over Emigrant Gap a day late, or perhaps she was commenting on the climb up Lowell Hill.

[12] Minerva Lester Power, "Letter to Mr. Davis," 8 October 1851. In this letter, Power also confirms her grandparents came to Nevada City "by way of Bear Valley."

[13] The Davises may have taken the Nevada City route and not the Bear River route. If we assume the Davises spent the night of the fourteenth and not the thirteenth in Bear Valley, perhaps slowed by the very rough trail conditions after crossing Roller Pass, then Sarah's "mile up and mile down" comment is placed in better context with Emigrant Gap. From their Bear Valley camp on the fourteenth, two days travel (the fifteenth and seventeenth) along the Nevada City route would then easily put the Davises in Nevada City. On the other hand, this argument doesn't account very well for Sarah's and Power's assertions that the Davises spent the night of the fifteenth and sixteenth in "bear valey to grasse our cattle." If Sarah was mistaken about her Bear River location on the sixteenth, then the argument that they took the Nevada City route is the stronger. But since Sarah did fix the party in Bear Valley on the sixteenth, I believe that it was more probable that the Davises took the Bear River route.

[14] Don Buck provided the description of the path out of Bear Valley to Deadmans Flat.

[15] Newell, 275, 277. Newell quotes several emigrants (Augustus Burbank, 1849; Charles Park, 1849; and Charles Long, 1849) who all refer to the Greenhorn Creek as the Bear River or Little Bear River.

[16] Ibid., 274, 275.

[17] Power, "Letter to Mr. Davis."

Chapter Six
Epilogue

After arriving in Nevada City, the Davises remained in Mr. Pottenger's unfinished cabin on the southwest corner of Pine and Spring Streets for about three weeks until construction on a nearby house was completed. They moved into this new home in early November. In 1851, the Davises moved again, this time into a boarding house. Later the same year, the Davises purchased, moved into, and ran another boarding house adjacent to the National Hotel. Then in 1853, the Davises built a house behind the National Hotel, on the south side of Spring Street. They spent the rest of their lives in this home.[1]

After the initial settling into Nevada City, Zeno established a gunsmith shop adjacent to his home on Spring Street.[2] Zeno was involved in real estate; active in local politics, serving as a town trustee in 1856;[3] the president of a mining claim;[4] and an inventor (there are scraps of evidence suggesting he had a hand in the invention or improvements of both the Pelton wheel and the hydraulic monitor).[5] On 17 June 1902, Zeno died from "old age" in Nevada City, aged eighty-three.[6] At the time of his death, he had been married to Sarah for fifty-eight years.

Sarah Ann's child survived the trip only to die soon after arriving in Nevada City. Minerva Power states, "the milk of the cows was poor after the long trip and it did not agree with [the baby], although they got milk from other cows on arriving but it could not stand it."[7] There are no other records concerning the child.

Cleora was raised in Nevada City and attended "the old Nevada Brick High School."[8] Her four surviving monthly high school report cards reflect an energetic (thirty-one demerits) and able student, while her high school compositions reflect an inquisitive and thoughtful mind, with one titled "The Ladies of France" and another titled "Time."[9] She married Anson Wood Lester on 5 May 1869 when she was nineteen years old.[10] Cleora had two children, Minerva and Fredrick S. Lester. In 1876, the death of Anson precipitated Cleora moving back in with Zeno and Sarah on Spring Street.[11] She became a successful partner in a fashionable Broad Street hat and bonnet shop.[12] Cleora remained in Nevada City until an advanced age, then moved in with her daughter, Minerva, who had married and moved to San Francisco.[13] On 11 June 1939, Cleora died in San Francisco, aged eighty-nine.[14]

In 1852, Sarah gave birth to Elbridge. Elbridge became a printer, married Addie I. Gray, fathered a son, James Rudd Davis (the author's grandfather), and, unfortunately, died early at forty-one years.[15]

It is unclear what became of Alexander. There is some indication he became a butcher in the nearby town of Grass Valley.[16] Other documents have Alexander as a building contractor in Nevada City.[17] Alexander died, probably in the 1890s, in California.[18]

Zeno's younger brother, Edwin, probably worked the mines for a number of years before moving on to Kelseyville, California, where he was granted 160 acres of land as part of the Homestead Act.[19] He died near Kelseyville at the Lakeport County Hospital in 1895 and is buried in Lakeport's Hartley Cemetery.[20]

Unfortunately, there was little done to record the events of Sarah's life after she stopped recording it for herself—it seems the activities of women in the latter half of the nineteenth century were ill recorded. Nevertheless, she raised the children and dealt with the moves, fires, and turbulence of frontier town life in the mining hills of California. She survived her son and her husband before her death on 5 December 1906 in Nevada City, aged eighty.[21]

Figure 29. Sarah and Zeno Davis in 1901. (From the private collection of Susan (Davis) Sutter.)

Notes

[1] Minerva Lester Power, "Early Business Locations of Z. P. Davis, Including the National Hotel, Information Given By Him [to Minerva Power] in 1899" (unpublished, May 1930).

[2] Shelton, 80.

[3] N. P. Brown and J. K. Dallison, *Brown & Dallison's Nevada, Grass Valley and Rough and Ready Directory, for the Year Commencing January 1st, 1856* (San Francisco, CA: Printed at the Town Talk Office, 1856), 124.

[4] Z. P. Davis, "The Willow Mining Company," The Nevada Democrat (Nevada City, CA), February 11, 1857, 2.

[5] Minerva Lester Power, "Untitled Note Referencing the Hydraulic Monitor," n.d., The Bancroft Library, Berkeley, CA; Edwin Tyson, "Pioneer Diaries," Nevada County Historical Society, October 1999, 2. The Bancroft Library at the University of California, Berkeley, is home to a collection of Anson W. Lester's private papers including the above note (collection name: Lester (A.W.) Family Papers, box number BANC MSS C-B 759)

[6] Power, "Davis Family," 5; Unknown, "Record of Funeral," June 19, 1902.

[7] Davis, "Diary of Sarah Davis as Transcribed by Minerva L. Power," 24 June entry. Note by Power.

[8] Dixon Smith, "Zeno Philosopher Davis: Nevada City California Pioneer" (Unpublished, November 2003), 4.

[9] Two-dozen pages of Cleora's high school compositions reside at the Bancroft Library in Anson W. Lester's private papers (collection name: Lester (A.W.) Family Papers, box number BANC MSS C-B 759).

[10] David A. Comstock, *Nevada County Vital Statistics, 1850-1869 (and up to 1876 for Divorces): Births, Marriages, Separations, Divorces, Naturalizations, and Deaths in Nevada County, California, as Compiled from Cemeteries, Newspapers, Letters, Diaries, and Family Records* (Grass Valley, CA: Comstock Bonanza Press, 1986), DAVIS, Miss Addie entry.

[11] Smith, 4.

[12] Maria E. Brower, *Images of America: Nevada City* (Charleston, SC: Arcadia Publishing, 2005), 72.

[13] US Government, "United States Census, 1930, FamilySearch (https://familysearch.org/pal:/MM9.1.1/XC6Y-CN6 : Accessed 08 Sep 2012), E Barnum Power, San Francisco (Districts 1-250), San Francisco,

California; Citing Enumeration District (ED) 0153, Sheet 4A, Family 65, NARA Microfilm Publication T626, Roll 200," 1930. E. Barnum Power was Minerva's husband.

[14] Power, "Davis Family," 5.

[15] Mathews, 247. It is interesting to note that "Rudd" was a prominent family in Cass County when Sarah and Zeno left there. Lydia, Sarah's sister, would marry Stephen Rudd and remain in Cass County.

[16] Brown and Dallison, 114.

[17] Power, "Davis Family," 5; Power, "Early Business Locations of Z. P. Davis." In "Early Business Locations," Power states that "In 1854 Mr. Davis built the upper or older portion of the present National Hotel…his brother Alexander Davis being the contractor."

[18] Power, "Davis Family," 5.

[19] Edwin F. Bean, *Bean's History and Directory of Nevada County, California* (California: Daily Gazette Book and Job Office, 1867), 254; US Bureau of Land Management, "Home - BLM GLO Records", n.d.

[20] Power, "Davis Family," 5; Anita Crabtree, "Edwin Davis," telephone interview, 24 February 2012. Ms. Crabtree is a representative of the Lake County, California, Genealogical Society.

[21] "Mrs. Sarah Davis Is Dead: Pioneer Women [sic] Succumbed Last Night," The Daily Union (Nevada City, CA), December 6, 1906.

Bibliography

Bancroft, Hubert H. *History of California.* 7 vols. San Francisco, CA: The History Company, 1884-90. http://www.books.google.com.

———. *History of the Pacific States of North America.* 34 vols. San Francisco, CA: A. L. Bancroft & Company, 1889-90. http://www. books.google.com.

Bean, Edwin F. *Bean's History and Directory of Nevada County, California.* California: Daily Gazette Book and Job Office, 1867. http://www.google.books.com/.

Benke, Arthur C., and Colbert E. Cushing. *Rivers of North America.* London: Elsevier, 2005.

Bigelow, John. *Memoir of the Life and Public Services of John Charles Frémont.* New York: Derby & Jackson, 1856. http://www.google. books.com/.

Bishop, L. C. "Wyoming Historical Maps | Wyoming State Historical Society." *L. C. Bishop Emigrant Trail Map Series*, n.d., http:// wyshs.org/node/35.

Black, Bob, Linda Black, and Larry Schmidt. *Hastings Cutoff & Pack Trails Driving Guide.* Reno, NV: Trails West, Inc., 2010.

Blackmar, Frank W. *Kansas: A Cyclopedia of State History, Embracing Events, Institutions, Industries, Counties, Cities, Towns, Prominent Persons, Etc.* 2 vols. Chicago, IL: Standard Publishing Co., 1912. http://www.books.google.com/books/about/Kansas. html?id=o8X5krq3fP8C

Boren, Ray. "Restored Site a Repository for Tooele's History." *Deseret News.* Salt Lake City, UT, September 18, 1997. http://www. deseretnews.com/article/583652/Restored-site-a-repository-for-Tooeles-history.html.

Bourne, Russell. *Floating West: The Erie and Other American Canals.* 1st ed. New York: Norton, 1992.

Brands, H. W. *The Age of Gold: The California Gold Rush and the New American Dream.* New York: Doubleday, 2002.

Bresee, Floyd, E. "Overland Freighting in the Platte Valley 1850-1870." Master's thesis, University of Nebraska, 1937. http://digitalcommons.unl.edu/cgi/viewcontent. cgi?article=1003&context=historydiss.

Brock, Richard K. and Donald E. Buck. *A Guide to the California Trail along the Humboldt River.* 2nd ed. Reno, NV: Trails West, Inc., 2007.

Brower, Maria E. *Images of America: Nevada City*. Charleston, SC: Arcadia Publishing, 2005.

Brown, N. P., and J. K. Dallison. *Brown & Dallison's Nevada, Grass Valley and Rough and Ready Directory, for the Year Commencing January 1st, 1856*. San Francisco, CA: Printed at the Town Talk Office, 1856. http://www.books.google.com.

Bryant, Edwin. *What I Saw in California*. 3rd ed. New York: D. Appleton & Company, 1849. http://www.books.google.com/.

Burdick, Charles W. *The State of Wyoming: An Official Publication Containing Reliable Information Concerning the Resources of the State*. State of Wyoming, 1898. http://www.books.google.com.

CA State Mining Bureau. "Placer County California." Topographical. CA: California State Mining Bureau, 1902. http://hdl.loc.gov/loc.gmd/g4363p.ct001904.

Cain, Joseph. "Letter of Joseph Cain." *Deseret News*. Salt Lake City, UT, October 5, 1850. http://archive.deseretnews.com/historic/.

Canfield, Chauncey L., ed. *The Diary of a Forty-Niner*. California Centennial. Stanford, CA: James Ladd Delkin, 1947.

"Cass County Marriages, Liber B," n.d., Cass District Library, Local History Branch, Genealogy and Research, Cassopolis, MI.

Caughey, John. *The California Gold Rush*. 1948. Paperback ed. Berkeley, CA: University of California Press, 1975.

Child, Andrew. *Overland Route to California*. Milwaukee: Daily Sentinel Steam Power Press, 1852. Reprint, Los Angeles: N. A. Kovach, 1946.

Christensen, Lawrence O., ed. *Dictionary of Missouri Biography*. Columbia, MO: University of Missouri Press, 1999.

Clayton, William. *The Latter-Day Saints' Emigrants' Guide*. St. Louis, MO: Republican Steam Power Press, Chambers & Knapp, 1848. http://www.archive.org/details/latterdaysaintse00clay.

Clemens, Natalie. "Down by the Old Mill." *Desert News*. Salt Lake City, UT, July 15, 2005. http://www.desertnews.com/article/600147472/Down-by-the-old-mill.html.

Colton, G. Woolworth. "Map of the United States of America," 1850. http://hdl.loc.gov/loc.gmd/g3700.ct000761.

Colton, John H. *The Western Tourist and Emigrant's Guide*. New York: J. H. Colton and Company, 1855. http://name.umdl.umich.edu/aja3435.0001.001.

Comstock, David A. *Brides of the Gold Rush*. 2nd ed. Grass Valley, CA: Comstock Bonanza Press, 2000.

———. *Nevada County Vital Statistics, 1850-1869 (and up to 1876 for Divorces): Births, Marriages, Separations, Divorces, Naturalizations, and Deaths in Nevada County, California, as Compiled from Cemeteries, Newspapers, Letters, Diaries, and Family Records*. Grass Valley, CA: Comstock Bonanza Press, 1986.

———. *News and Advertising in the Early Gold Camps of Nevada County, California*. Grass Valley, CA: Comstock Bonanza Press, 2008.

The Daily Union. "Mrs. Sarah Davis Is Dead: Pioneer Women [sic] Succumbed Last Night." Nevada City, CA, December 6, 1906.

Davis, Sarah. "Diary of Sarah Davis." Yale Collection of Western Americana, Beinecke Rare Book and Manuscript Library, Yale University, 1850.

———. "Diary of Sarah Davis as Transcribed by Minerva L. Power." Edited by Minerva Lester Power, ca. 1940.

Davis, Z. P. "The Willow Mining Company." *The Nevada Democrat*. Nevada City, CA, February 11, 1857.

DeLorme Mapping Company. "California Atlas & Gazetteer." Yarmouth, ME: DeLorme, 2008.

———. "Nevada Atlas & Gazetteer." Yarmouth, ME: DeLorme, 2001.

Dodge, G. M. "Map of the Union Pacific Rail Road and Surveys of 1864, 65, 66, 67, 1868 from Missouri River to Humboldt Wells." Topographical. H. Lambach, 1869. Library of Congress. g4051p rr005920 http://hdl.loc.gov/loc.gmd/g4051p.rr005920.

Donovan, Frank. *River Boats of America*. 1st ed. New York: Thomas Y. Crowell Company, 1966.

Drago, Harry S. *The Steamboaters: From the Early Side-Wheelers to the Big Packets*. 1st ed. New York: Bramhall House, 1967.

Drury, George. *The Historical Guide to North American Railroads*. Milwaukee: Kalmbach Books, 1985.

Dunbar, Seymour. *History of Travel in America*. New ed. New York: Tudor, 1937.

Egloffstein, F. W. "From Great Salt Lake to the Humboldt Mountains. From Explorations and Surveys Made Under the Direction of the Hon. Jefferson Davis, Secretary of War by Capt. E. G. P. Beckwith, 3d. Artillery. E. [sic] W. Egloffstein, Topographer for the Route, 1855." Topographical. Washington, DC: Selmar Siebert's Engraving & Printing Establishment, 1859. http://hdl. loc.gov/loc.gmd/g4341p.rr001660.

Espenshade, Edward B., Jr., ed. *Goode's World Atlas*. 16th ed. Chicago: Rand McNally & Company, 1982.

Fagan, Brian. *The Little Ice Age: The Prelude to Global Warming 1300-1850*. Boulder, CO: Basic Books, 2000.

Fenneman, N. M., and D. W. Johnson. *Physiographic Divisions of the Conterminous U.S.* Washington, DC: US Geological Survey, 2011. http://www.data.gov/geodata/g601660/.

Ferris, Warren A. "Warren A. Ferris's Map of the Northern Rockies." Topographical. Utah State Historical Society, 2009. http://content.lib.utah.edu/cdm4/item_viewer.php?CISOROOT=%-2FUSHS_Class&CISOPTR=21407&DMSCALE=50.00000&D-MWIDTH=700&DMHEIGHT=700&DMMODE=viewer&DM-FULL=0&DMOLDSCALE=5.79151&DMX=0&DMY=0&DM-TEXT=&DMTHUMB=1&REC=1&DMROTATE=0&x=101&y=25.

Fradkin, Philip L. *Sagebrush Country: Land and the American West*. Reprint, Komph. Boulder, CO: Johnson Books, 2004.

Franzwa, Gregory. *Maps of the California Trail*. Tucson, AZ: Patrice Press, 1999.

———. *Maps of the Oregon Trail*. St. Louis, MO: Patrice Press, 1990.

Freeman, Christine. "Alphabetical Listing of People and Some Buildings and Events of Special Significance," n.d. Doris Foley Historical Library, Nevada City, CA.

Frémont, J. C. *Memoirs of My Life*. 1st Cooper Square Press ed. New York [Lanham, MD]: Cooper Square Press; Distributed by National Book Network, 2001.

Gilbert, Grove Karl. *Lake Bonneville*. Washington, DC: US Government, 1890. http://archive.org/details/lakebonneville00gilb.

Golay, Michael, and John S. Bowman. *North American Exploration*. Edison, NJ: Castle Books, 2006.

Goode, Harry D. *Thermal Waters of Utah, Topical Report*. Salt Lake City, UT: Utah Geological and Mineral Survey, 1978. http://digitalcommons.usu.edu/govdocs/33.

Gowans, Fred, and Eugene Campbell. *Fort Bridger, Island in the Wilderness*. Provo, UT: Brigham Young University Press, 1975.

"Great Register of Nevada County," 1892. Doris Foley Historical Library, Nevada City, CA.

Hastings, Lansford W. *The Emigrant's Guide to Oregon and California*. Applewood Books, 1994. http://www.books.google.com/.

Hinshaw, William Wade. *Encyclopedia of American Quaker Genealogy*. 6 vols. Baltimore: Genealogical Pub. Co., 1969.

Holliday, J. S. *The World Rushed In: The California Gold Rush Experience*. Red River Books. Norman, OK: University of Oklahoma Press, 2002.

Holmes, Kenneth L. *Covered Wagon Women: Diaries & Letters from the Western Trails, 1840-1849*. 11 vols. Bison Book Ed. Glendale, CA: Arthur H. Clark Company, 1983. Reprint, Lincoln, NE: University of Nebraska Press, 1995.

Howard, Thomas F. *Sierra Crossing: First Roads to California*. Berkeley, CA: University of California Press, 1998.

Hunter, Louis C., and Beatrice Jones Hunter. *Steamboats on the Western Rivers: An Economic and Technological History*. Mineola, NY: Dover, 1993.

Hunter, Milton R. *Brigham Young the Colonizer*. Kessinger Publishing, 2004. www.books.google.com.

Illinois. "Harvesting the River: Transportation: Boats: Steamboats — Illinois State Museum," n.d. http://www.museum.state.il.us/ RiverWeb/harvesting/transportation/boats/steamboats.html.

Jackson, W. *Wagon Roads West: A Study of Federal Road Surveys and Construction in the Trans-Mississippi West, 1864-1869*. Lincoln, NE: University of Nebraska Press, 1979.

Jefferson, T. H. "Map of the Emigrant Road from Independence Mo. to St. Francisco California." Topographical. New York: T. H. Jefferson, 1849. Library of Congress. http://hdl.loc.gov/loc. gmd/g4051p.tr000113.

Jervis, John B. "Map of the Northwestern States." Outline Map. New York: Lithograph: Wm Endicott & Co., 1850. http://hdl.loc.gov/ loc.gmd/g4071p.rr001160.

Kelley, Charles. *Salt Desert Trails: A History of the Hastings Cutoff and Other Early Trails Which Crossed the Great Salt Desert Seeking a Shorter Road to California*. Salt Lake City, UT: Western Printing Co., 1930.

Kern, Edward M. "Journal of Edward Kern (1845)." *The Nevada Observer Reading Room*, n.d. http://www.nevadaobserver. com/Reading%20Room%20Documents/journal_of_edward_ kern_1845.htm.

Korns, J. Roderic, and Dale Lowell Morgan. *West from Fort Bridger: The Pioneering of the Immigrant Trails Across Utah, 1846-1850.* Logan, UT: Utah State Historical Society, 1951. Reprint, Logan, UT: Utah State University Press, 1994.

Laut, Agnes C. *The Overland Trail: The Epic Path of the Pioneers to Oregon.* New York: Grosset & Dunlap, 1929.

Lavender, David. *The Overland Migrations: Settlers to Oregon, California, and Utah.* Washington, DC: US Department of the Interior, 1980.

Leicht, Ferdinand von. "Topographical Map of Lake Tahoe and Surrounding Country." Topographical. San Francisco, 1874. http://memory.loc.gov/cgi-bin/map_item.pl.

Leonard, Glen. "Farmington." *Utah History Encyclopedia.* Salt Lake City, UT: The State of Utah, 2011. http;//historytogo.utah.gov/places/farmington.html.

Lester, A. W. "Lester (A.W.) Family Papers, [1853-ca. 1910]." *Online Archive of California,* n.d. Collection name: Lester (A.W.) Family Papers, box number BANC MSS C-B 759. http://www.oac.cdlib.org/

Lester, Cleora. "Pioneer of 1850 Tells of Her Coming to California." *The Morning Union.* Nevada City, CA, October 21, 1924.

Lienhard, Heinrich. *From St. Louis to Sutter's Fort, 1846.* Translated by Erwin G. Gudde and Elisabeth K. Gudde. The American Exploration and Travel Series. Norman, OK: University of Oklahoma Press, 1961.

Lobeck, A. K. "Geologic Map of the United States." New Jersey: Hamond, 1966.

Mann, Michael E. "Little Ice Age." In *Encyclopedia of Global Environmental Change,* edited by Michael D. MacCracken and John S. Perry. Chichester: Wiley, 2002. http://www.meteo.psu.edu/.

Massey, Rheba. *Transportation: Trails Context.* Wyoming: State of Wyoming, 1992. http://wyoshpo.state.wy.us/pdf/transpor.pdf.

Mathews, Alfred. *History of Cass County, Michigan: With Illustrations and Biographical Sketches of Some of Its Prominent Men and Pioneers.* Chicago, IL: Waterman, Watkins & Co., 1882. Reprint, Evansville, IN: Unigraphic, Inc., 1971. Reprint, Lansing, MI: Inter-Collegiate Press Service Center, 1985.

Mattes, Merrill J. *The Great Platte River Road: The Covered Wagon Mainline Via Fort Kearny to Fort Laramie.* 2nd ed. Lincoln, NE: University of Nebraska Press, 1969.

McBride, John P. "Pioneer Days in the Mountains." *Tullidge's Quarterly Magazine*, October 1883. http//books.google.com/.

McLynn, Frank. *Wagons West: The Epic Story of America's Overland Trails.* 1st American ed. New York: Grove Press, 2002.

Meldahl, Keith. *Hard Road West: History & Geology Along the Gold Rush Trail.* Chicago, IL: University of Chicago Press, 2007.

Missouri Immigration Society. *Hand-Book of Missouri.* St. Louis, MO: Times Printing House, 1880. http://www.books.google.com.

Moorman, Madison Berryman. *The Journal of Madison Berryman Moorman, 1850-1851.* Edited by Irene D. Paden. San Francisco, CA: California Historical Society, 1948.

Morgan, Dale Lowell. *Jedediah Smith and the Opening of the West.* Second Bison ed. Lincoln, NE: Bison Books, 1964.

Newell, Olive. *Tail of the Elephant: The Emigrant Experience on the Truckee Route of the California Trail 1844-1842.* Nevada City, CA: Nevada County Historical Society, 1997.

"NPS Historical Handbook: Scotts Bluff", n.d. http://www.cr.nps.gov/history/online_books/hh/28/hh28l.htm.

O'Hanlon, John, and Edward J. Maguire. *Reverend John O'Hanlon's The Irish Emigrant's Guide for the United States.* Stratford, NH: Ayer Publishing, 1976. http://www.books.google.com.

Ohio Historical Society. "Roster of Ohio Soldiers in the War of 1812," n.d. http://www.ohiohistory.org/onlinedoc/militaryroster/1812/txt/page0049.txt.

Oudergeest, Bill. "What Do We Do Now?" *Donner Summit Historical Society Newsletter*, 2011. www.donnersummithistoricalsociety.org%2FPDFs%2Fnewsletters%2Fnews11%2Fnovember11.pdf&ei=xGAET9.

Paden, Irene D. *Prairie Schooner Detours.* New York: The Macmillan Company, 1949.

———. *The Wake of the Prairie Schooner.* New York: The Macmillan Company, 1943.

Palmer, Joel. *Journal of Travels Over the Rocky Mountains.* Cincinnati: J.A. & U.P. James, 1847. Reprint, Fairfield, WA: Ye Galleon Press, 1983. http://www.books.google.com/.

Peoria Regional Museum Society. "A Most Glorious Power: A History of Early Steam Engine Use and Manufacture in Peoria, Illinois Area." *Peoria Regional Museum Society*, 2011. http:// peoriahistory.org/History-of-the-Steam-Engine-in-Peoria,-IL. php.

Peoria, Ill. "Advertisement for the River Boat 'Mungo Park' in the Peoria City Directory," 1844. http://peoriahistory.org/images/ Steam_images_large/IMG_087.jpg.

Phelps, Humphrey. *Phelps Travellers' Guide Through the United States.* New York: Ensigns & Thayer, 1850. http://railroads.unl.edu/ documents/view_document.php?id=rail.PTG1850.

Power, Minerva Lester. "Davis Family." Unpublished, September 20, 1942.

———. "Early Business Locations of Z. P. Davis, Including the National Hotel, Information Given By Him [to Minerva Power] in 1899." Unpublished, 1930.

———. "Letter to Mr. Davis." October 8, 1851. Searls Library, Nevada City, CA.

———. "Untitled Note Referencing the Hydraulic Monitor," n.d. The Bancroft Library, Berkeley, CA.

Preuss, Charles. *Exploring with Frémont: The Private Diaries of Charles Preuss, Cartographer for John C. Frémont on His First, Second, and Fourth Expeditions to the Far West.* Translated by Erwin G. Gudde and Elisabeth K. Gudde. Norman, OK: University of Oklahoma Press, 1958.

———. "Map of an Exploring Expedition to the Rocky Mountains in the Year 1842 and to Oregon & North California in the Years 1843-44." Topographical. Baltimore: E. Weber & Co, 1845. http://hdl.loc.gov/loc.gmd/g4051s.ct000909.

———. "Map of an Exploring Expedition to the Rocky Mountains in the Year 1842, Oregon and North California in the Years 1843-44. With Annotations of George Gibbs," n.d. http://www.wdl.org/ en/item/6768/.

———. "Topographical Map of the Road from Missouri to Oregon, Commencing at the Mouth of the Kansas in the Missouri River and Ending at the Mouth of the Walla-Wallah in the Columbia." Topographical. Baltimore: E. Weber & Co, 1846. http://hdl.loc. gov/loc.gmd/g4127o.mf000048.

———. "Map of Oregon and Upper California from the Surveys of John Charles Frémont and Other Authorities." Topographical. Washington, DC: US Senate, 1848. Library of Congress. http://hdl.loc.gov/loc.gmd/g4210.ct000910.

Raisz, Erwin. "Landforms of the United States." Topographical, 1957.

Rasmussen, Louis J. *California Wagon Train Lists*. Colma, CA: San Francisco Historic Records, 1994.

Rosenbert, Don. "Utah History Resource Center." *Markers and Monuments Database*, n.d. http://history.utah.gov/apps/markers/detailed_results.php?markerid=1491.

Safra, Jacob E., ed. "Bridger, Jim." *The New Encyclopaedia Britannica*. Chicago: Encyclopædia Britannica, 2005.

Scrugham, James G. "Nevada: The Narrative of the Conquest of a Frontier Land." *The Nevada Observer*, December 10, 2006. http://www.nevadaobserver.com/.

Settle, Raymond W., and Mary Lund Settle. *Empire on Wheels*. Stanford, CA: Stanford University Press, 1949.

———. "The Early Careers of William Bradford Waddell and William Hepburn Russell: Frontier Capitalists." *The Kansas Historical Quarterly*, Winter 1960, 355–382.

Shelton, Lawrence P. *California Gunsmiths 1846-1900*. Fair Oaks, CA: Far West Publishers, 1977.

Simpson, J. H. "Map of Wagon Routes in Utah Territory Explored & Opened by Capt. J. H. Simpson Topographical Engineers U.S.A." Topographical. US Government, 1859. http://hdl.loc.gov/loc.gmd/g4341p.ct003103.

Smith, Calvin J. "Guide Through Ohio, Michigan, Indiana, Illinois, Missouri, Wisconsin & Iowa." New York: J. H. Colton, 1844. http://memory.loc.gov/.

Smith, Jedediah. "Jedediah Smith's Journals," n.d. http://mtmen.org/mtman/html/jsmith/index.html.

Spence, Mary Lee, and Donald Jackson, eds. *The Expeditions of John Charles Frémont*. Vol. II. Urbana, IL: University of Illinois Press, 1973. http://www.archive.org/stream/expeditionsofjoh02fr/expeditionsofjoh02fr_djvu.txt.

Stansbury, Howard, and J. W. Gunnison. "Map of the Great Salt Lake and Adjacent Country in the Territory of Utah (Surveyed in 1849 and 1850)." Topographical. New York: Akerman Lith., 1851. http://memory.loc.gov/.

State of Nevada. "Carson River Chronology," n.d. http://water. nv.gov/mapping/chronologies/carson/part2.cfm.

State of Wyoming. "The Emigrant Trails in Wyoming," n.d. http:// wyoshpo.state.wy.us/trailsdemo/.

———. "Wyoming Cultural Resource Information System (WYCRIS) / On-line Research," n.d. http://wyoshpo.state.wy.us/ OLResources/Index.aspx.

Steele, John. *Across the Plains in 1850*. Chicago: Printed for the Caxton Club, 1930.

Stewart, George R. *The California Trail: An Epic with Many Heroes*. 1st ed. The American Trails Series. New York: McGraw-Hill, 1962.

Tea, Roy D. "'Hastings Longtrip': A Hastings Cutoff Trail Guide from Donner Spring to the Humboldt River." Salt Lake City, UT, 1996.

———. "The Hastings Cutoff Across Utah: The Donner/Reed Party & Other Emigrants 1846-50." *The Hastings Cutoff Across Utah*, n.d. http://www.scienceviews.com/historical/hastingstext.html.

———. "The Hastings Cutoff: Grantsville to Donner Springs." Salt Lake City, UT, 1996.

Tullidge, Edward William. *Tullidge's Histories*. 2 vols. Salt Lake City, UT: Press of the Juvenile Instructor, 1889. http://www.books. google.com/.

Tyson, Edwin. "Pioneer Diaries." *Nevada County Historical Society*, October 1999.

University of Nebraska. "Digging In: The Historic Trails of Nebraska," n.d. http://cdrh.unl.edu/diggingin/.

Unknown. "Record of Funeral," June 19, 1902.

Unruh, John D., Jr. *The Plains Across: The Overland Emigrants and the Trans-Mississippi West, 1840-60*. 1st unabridged paperback edition, 1993. Urbana, IL: University of Illinois Press, 1979.

US Bureau of Land Management. "Home - BLM GLO Records," n.d. http://www.glorecords.blm.gov/.

———. "Oregon Trail Education Resource Guide." Bureau of Land Management, n.d. www.blm.gov/or/oregontrail/files/TBKS_ opt.pdf.

———. "Tour the Trails," n.d. http://www.blm.gov/wy/st/en/ programs/nlcs/Historic_Trails/trails_tour.html#ot.

———. "US Department of the Interior Bureau of Land Management," 2011. http://www.blm.gov/wy/st/en/ resources/public_room/gis/datagis.html.

US Department of Agriculture. "Trails Information," n.d. http:// www.fs.fed.us/recreation/programs/trails/.

US Department of the Interior. *National Historic Trails Auto Tour Route Interpretive Guide across Wyoming*. Salt Lake City, UT: National Park Service, 2007.

US Geological Survey. "California Colfax Sheet." Topographical. US Government, 1891.

———. "Cokeville." Topographical. US Government, 1967.

———. "Jiggs Nevada." Topographical. US Government, 1931.

———. "Norden." Topographical. US Government, 2000.

———. "Quincy Spring." Topographical. U.S. Government, 1973.

———. "St. Joseph, MO." Topographical. Washington, DC: US Geological Survey, 1926. University of Texas. http://www.lib. utexas.edu/maps/topo/missouri/pclmaps-topo-mo-saint-joseph-1924.jpg.

———. "Sublet." Topographical. US Government, 1985.

———. "The National Map," n.d. http://nationalmap.gov/viewers. html.

———. "Tooele." Topographical. US Government, 1976.

———. "Truckee." Topographical. US Government, 1895.

———. "US Board on Geographic Names," 2011. http://geonames. usgs.gov/index.html.

US Government. "Prints & Photographs Online Catalog," n.d. http://www.loc.gov/pictures/.

———. "United States Census, 1930, FamilySearch (https:// familysearch.org/pal:/MM9.1.1/XC6Y-CN6: Accessed 08 Sep 2012), E Barnum Power, San Francisco (Districts 1-250), San Francisco, California; Citing Enumeration District (ED) 0153, Sheet 4A, Family 65, NARA Microfilm Publication T626, Roll 200." 1930.

US National Park Service. "California National Historic Trail - Brochures (US National Park Service)," 2007. http://www.nps. gov/cali/planyourvisit/brochures.htm.

———. *California National Historic Trails Comprehensive Management and Use Plan: Final Environmental Impact Statement*. United States Department of the Interior, 1998.

———. "Illinois & Michigan Canal National Heritage Corridor (National Park Service)," 1984. http://www.nps.gov/ilmi/ index.htm.

———. "Mormon Pioneer National Historic Trail," n.d. http://www. cr.nps.gov/history/online_books/mopi/hrst.htm.

———. *National Historic Trails*, 2011. http://imgis.nps.gov/ArcGIS/ rest/services/NHT/NHT/MapServer/export?

US National Weather Service. "National Weather Service GIS Data Links," n.d. http://www.nws.noaa.gov/geodata/.

US Naval Observatory. "Complete Sun and Moon Data for One Day: Locations Worldwide — Naval Oceanography Portal," 2011. http://www.usno.navy.mil/USNO/astronomical-applications/ data-services/rs-one-day-world.

US Senate. *Resolution Introduced by Senator Henry Clay in Relation to the Adjustment of All Existing Questions of Controversy Between the States Arising Out of the Institution of Slavery (The Compromise of 1850), January 29, 1850*, 1850. http://www.ourdocuments.gov/.

Utley, Robert Marshall. *A Life Wild and Perilous*. New York: Henry Holt & Co., 1997.

Walker, William Z. "Diary of William Walker." Provo, UT, 1949. http://www.memory.loc.gov digital ID: upbover dia1182.

Ware, Joseph E. *The Emigrant's Guide to California*. St. Louis, MO: Union Office, 1849. Reprint, New Jersey: Princeton University Press, 1932. Reprint, New York: De Capo Press, 1972.

Wells, Harry L. *History of Nevada County, California*. Oakland, CA: Thompson & West, 1880. Reprint, with introduction by W. Turrentine Jackson. Berkeley, CA: Howell North Books, 1970.

West, Daniel B. "Daniel B. West - Diary 1850," 1850. http://www. tinyvital.com/Misc/Daniel_West_1850_Diary.html.

Willoughby, Robert J. *The Great Western Migration to the Gold Fields of California, 1849-1850*. Jefferson, NC: McFarland & Company, Inc., 2003.

Wishart, David J., ed. "Oregon Trail." *Encyclopedia of the Great Plains*. Lincoln, NE: The University of Nebraska, 2011. http:// plainshumanities.unl.edu/encyclopedia/.

Wood, Julia Newton. "Diary of Mrs. Julia Newton Wood 1853." Accessed December 29, 2012. http://www.geckodance.com/ oregontrail/diary1853.html.

Made in the USA
Monee, IL
07 July 2026